FIGHT OR FLIGHT!

Make better decisions to enjoy your life

GREGORY B. DAVIS

Fight or Flight! Make better decisions to enjoy your life - First Edition

Design by RLS Creativity

ISBN (epub) 978-1-734643-0-4

ISBN (print) 978-1-734643-1-1

Grateful

I'm grateful for my family.

I feel that I'm standing next to and on the shoulders of giants. The support of my family is vital to every part of my book. They've had my back since I was born all the way to reading and rereading version after version of Fight or Flight! Make better decisions to enjoy your life. I'm humbled to be associate with such a loving and quality group.

"My will and reason were powerless against the imagination of a danger **which had never been experienced**."

— CHARLES DARWIN (EMPHASIS MINE)

CONTENTS

PART 1: WHAT IS FIGHT OR FLIGHT

PART 2: FIGHT OR FLIGHT AND OUR HEALTH

PART 3: FIGHT OR FLIGHT IMPACT ON YOU

PART 4: THE END OF FIGHT OR FLIGHT

INTRODUCTION

Imagine yourself as a boxer. You're standing in the middle of the ring. Logically, you know blows are coming your way, but you're not 100 percent clear on where they will come from and what type they will be. Now, tweak the image just a bit to see yourself in the ring of life. These left and right hooks become life events. You don't know what they'll be, or when they'll hit, but part of life is knowing that one event after another is coming your way and sometimes you might not feel ready. When these life events come to you, do you choose a Fight or Flight response? This mental simulation sets up our book.

At a few points in life, the Fight or Flight reaction might have saved you from terrible dangers, but on a daily basis, Fight or Flight is ruining your life.

A boxer is an ideal example of how to handle a Fight or Flight response. There is another individual in the ring who wants to physically harm the boxer and it is absolutely a fear-ful and dangerous situation. However, if boxers constantly stayed in a Fight or Flight frame of mind, they would exhaust themselves before the end of the fight in addition to setting up a poor short- and long-term decision-making environment.

Therefore, fighters train themselves to remain mentally calm and make the best decision possible for the next move in the fight—the ultimate goal for this book is to give you wisdom so that you can make good decisions for your life in Fight or Flight situations.

Trained boxers can see options when a threat is coming their way. They've trained themselves to counter the threat in many different manners. There is opportunity for success, opportunity to move into defense, and opportunity to stop the fight. Trained vs Untrained is the decision the world has to face in daily life. Wisdom is the beginning of leading a more successful, option-filled life.

For an untrained boxer, the experience is beyond exhausting, both mentally and physically. There is only instinctual reaction to what is coming at you in life. No planning, no possibility of looking at the options that lay before you. This combination makes for a bumpy life and relationships.

The same holds true for individuals in law enforcement. If they moved into Fight or Flight mode every time they heard a siren, they would not make effective decisions in difficult situations. They train themselves to see options when encountering the unknown.

In both situations, the fighter and the law enforcement officer know that the unknown is coming. They absolutely feel fear and know their body will start into a Fight or Flight response. More importantly, they also know it doesn't serve them well to stay there. They know the calmer, more logical and mentally prepared a situation they foster for themselves, the better their opportunity to create multiple viewpoints and best-case scenarios. Not only for themselves, but also for everyone involved.

You can be that trained boxer, that law officer in your own life, navigating one life event after another. Some events will come out of the blue, some you know are coming your way. When you can train yourself to stay calm (or just as important, regain calm) and see unlimited outcomes and possibilities, you win.

And this is my ultimate goal in this book for you and your life; that you have mental calmness so that you can make the best short- and long-term decision for yourself and loved ones when a fearful situation presents itself. With this book, it is also my hope that you take the first step to be a **trained** vs. an **untrained** boxer.

You will examine vital moments or steps in your decision-making process that ultimately take you to success versus regret. This is very important, since you will make millions of decisions in life, only a few of those are life-changing, and depending on how they are handled, the results could bring more of what you want in life or not.

Two key points in the decision-making process are the actual moment of reacting to life events and the subsequent moment when the decision is made.

We'll go over these points in detail so that next time you face them you will make the best decisions possible. You will be able to recognize them as they make your heart race, breath quicken, and when you experience butterflies in your stomach, among other reactions. What you do with them is what sets you apart from failure... and you will win!

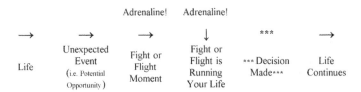

These life events and opportunities that get your hands sweaty and make your heart race often catch you off guard in the moment. You might dislike them at first, but these moments (over a lifetime) will set up and create an incredibly exciting life vs "just a life."

In order to live such an exciting, but successful life, it is key to make great decisions during what we might consider difficult times. It is a challenge to think when you are caught off guard by a life event or potential life event (like having to give a speech to your colleagues). Your helpful body kicks into Fight or Flight mode, and a number of unhelpful things happen. Out of stress, bypassing this one opportunity may not have a huge impact on your life, but passing up opportunity after opportunity will.

This is what happens when life deals us a "blow" and our adrenal gland fires, mentally:

We Move to	We Give Up
Focus narrows	Opportunity to see big picture
Risk averse frame of mind	The mind-set of open and accepting
Make short-term decisions	Long-term successes
Formulate life or death conclusions	Life enhancement possibilities
Focus on negative outcomes	Positive states
Look to protect yourself	Opening yourself up

No doubt these all are very useful reactions when facing life or death situations. Alas, these are unhelpful when fighting with your spouse, when you've been offered a public speaking opportunity, or you're walking into a clinic for a doctor's appointment. They limit your participation in events outside of your comfort zone and drive you toward a scenario of "safety" which is the ultimate goal of the Flight or Flight response.

But do you really need to be safe from these daily situations? Living within the limitations of this primitive response puts all variables and futures states aside, leaving us with the known (**safe**) and ignoring the unknown (**potential**). This book is not about conquering your fears, but about understanding why you are afraid and deciding if the extent you've built up the fear is valid or not.

Some of your daily activities might trigger a Fight or Flight reaction—the world, your surroundings and media inputs—that project and communicate fear.

When you feel and experience lack of safety, your mind, instincts and senses pick up on it. Fear is valid, and Fight or Flight is normal, but when overdone, it will run and ruin your life. Steps must be taken to control this state of mind as swiftly as possible.

MY OWN EXPERIENCE

I was diagnosed with cancer when I was 33 years old. I had three surgeries and three rounds of chemotherapy. The chemo was particularly harsh for me. I had 5 days straight of 6- to 8-hour sessions, two weeks off, 5 more days of treatment and finally two weeks off and 5 days of treatment. To watch the chemo drugs drip into my IV and veins was mentally the most exhausting challenge I've ever faced.

As you can imagine, post-treatment check-ups are an important part of the treatment and recovery process. When I look back, the first few check-ups were non-events, as I was still in the blur of the diagnosis and treatments. Then over a year later, when I was returning to the clinic for follow-up, something interesting overcame my body as I entered the sliding door… it felt literally like a clear brick wall was in my face. As soon as the doors opened, as soon as the smell of cleaning products entered my nose, as soon as I saw the entrance to the chemo treatment room, I was back in time. My heart started to race, my stomach churned, my focus narrowed. My wife was holding my hand and I clearly remember her turning to me and asking if I was okay. She said "your palms are sweating."

My body was protecting itself and my Fight or Flight mechanism had kicked into "survival" mode. I'd mentally created a dangerous situation (unconsciously), and my response had taken over in that very moment. In that situation I (mentally) fought, pushed through the discomfort and attended the appointment. The discomfort and "danger" I'd faced over the preceding months had built up and my body felt as if it was entering into a Fight or Flight situation.

However, imagine if my trigger had been flying on planes, or all doctors or needles. Simply pushing through over the long term is not a healthy solution. This state is exhausting and may lead to an increased chance of making a decision that isn't ideal or the most healthy. Continuing with this line of thought, if the trigger is left unchecked, it can grow and become more and more of a blockade in life.

This blockade can greatly hinder healthy decisions, and by learning to gain control of these fearful thoughts, you can logically make better decisions for your life.

For me, I know that if I ever entered that clinic again, I would have the same physical reaction. Until I put my logical thinking brain back into control, I have the possibility of costing myself a really important check-up that could literally save my life.

What are your Fight or Flight triggering moments that currently run and ruin your life? Work on them throughout the book and you will make a better decision each time, moving forward.

WHO AM I?

I have a real passion for personal growth in my life. I enjoy helping and seeing people advance in life. I'm truly confident it makes life better for me and better for all those around me, and I trust that everyone has it within them to create a successful life on their own, starting today. I also know that as I share my life knowledge and insight, I can make the path of life more fruitful and less issue laden. Wisdom is the beginning, and life is too short to learn every life lesson ourselves, and so learning from others is the best way.

I've been very fortunate and have had the benefit of being part of a family who believed that personal growth was important. My grandmother and my parents started their own growth in the late 1970s and were deeply committed from the early 80s forward, up to today. My grandmother started a personal growth seminar (Choices Seminars) in the early 80s which still exists today and continues to work for the betterment of lives. She played a key role in the program, traveling every month, until she was in her early 80s! I grew up seeing her and my parents work the seminar rooms. Today I'm thankful to play my part and lead the seminars.

It keeps me sharp to be around people who chose to grow. By working with people daily and benefiting from my family's knowledge and experience, I've come to writing. This is not the first book I've written (more will come soon), but it is my first book to be published. I am proud and excited to play my part in passing on wisdom so the collective knowledge can grow.

I truly believe that Fight or Flight impacts us all and could make everyone's life better, when used constructively. I present my work and research here hoping that those who choose to read this book will have the tools to create more fullness in their life.

PART 1: WHAT IS FIGHT OR FLIGHT

OPENING STORY

As he walked into the meeting room and moved to the head of the table, he did a quick scan of the room. Everyone who needed to be there was in place. This was his moment. His time. He was ready. He had worked his whole life to get here. Overcome many obstacles. Spent countless late nights and weekends preparing for this very moment. His goal was in sight. The promotion was his. All he had to do was get through the presentation and then the Q&A.

He told himself not to think about the Q&A. He could feel his pulse quickening and his stomach rumbling each time the idea entered his mind. He focused on pulling the presentation up on the computer. It loaded immediately and appeared on the giant screen behind him at the front of the room. He didn't need to glance at it. He had tested it many times in preparation. He knew it was perfect.

He glanced down at his notes, looked back up at his peers and superiors, gave a welcoming smile, and pitched into his presentation. It was flawless. Exactly as he'd prepared for it to be.

And then the final slide appeared on the screen with its two ominous letters connected by an ampersand: Q&A.

It started, it hit him full force. No matter what he thought: *What if I cannot answer every question? What if someone knows more than I do? What if I look foolish in front of this entire room?*

The sweaty palms. The quickened heartbeat. The pounding in his head.

He took short, quick breaths. Reminding himself he was ready for anything. He knew his subject matter and his presentation backwards and forwards. Nobody could ask a question for which he didn't have the answer.

All the self-talk in the world didn't make a difference.

The first hand went up. He had a fraction of a second to propose a logical and accurate response or the room would turn against him. The first question was asked, and with it every answer, every bit of knowledge he held about his subject matter seemed to evaporate as his body flooded with adrenaline and his survival instincts kicked in with their screaming insistence that he should get out of there as fast as possible. He noticed his breath and thought, *Why am I holding my breath?*

Later he would reflect on the moment and feel the anger rising. Why did it always happen? It wasn't like he wasn't prepared or didn't know the answer. Why couldn't he stay present during the Q&A? And he'd promised himself it wouldn't happen again. Even though he knew it probably would. It was just the way he was wired, he told himself. He wondered if this only happened to him? Did this happen to others too? No matter how prepared he was, his brain froze and he wanted to run the moment he hit the Q&A segment of any presentation.

As he thought and rationalized, he made the decision to never put himself in a similar situation. He was never going to put himself out there again. At that point he settled for less in life.

HISTORY AND FACTS OF FIGHT OR FLIGHT

The theory of Fight or Flight was developed by Walter Bradford Cannon (he coined the phrase in his 1915 work, *Bodily Changes in Pain, Hunger, Fear and Rage: An Account of Recent Researches into the Function of Emotional Excitement*). In it, he states that "animals react to threats with a general discharge of the sympathetic nervous system, priming the animal for fighting or fleeing."

The Fight or Flight response can be traced to our adrenal glands. We have two small glands that sit above the kidneys which are responsible for an array of hormones and life functions. The gland interacts with the body by controlling and adjusting many functions, such as the ratio of sodium and potassium, sex hormones, metabolism, water balance and, of course, our response to fearful and dangerous situations.

The adrenal glands are fascinating; they perform a variety of duties for the body. The most fascinating part is that they can overperform their duties and, over time, become very harmful to our body and rob us of living the fullest life possible since we spend our days in a defensive mode. Some of the disorders which have been identified are Cushings Syndrome (when too much cortisol is produced) and Addison's Disease (too little cortisol is produced).

For this book's purposes, let's focus on the adrenal gland from the role it plays in the Fight or Flight response. Specifically, how it impacts our mental thoughts and decision-making process. First, let's see in detail what happens to our body, step by step, when we experience Fight or Flight:

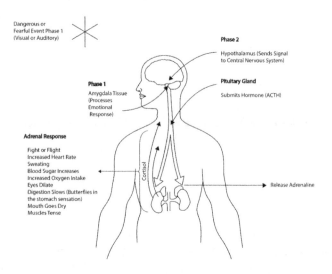

Diagram notes: This simple diagram demonstrates some of the body's reaction during the Fight or Flight response. There are additional aspects of the responses such as when the adrenaline subsides in the body, the hypothalamus may activate another component of the response which releases corticotropin-releasing hormone (CRH) and then cortisol. This keeps the Fight or Flight response engaged as long as the hypothalamus experiences Fear or Danger. 1 1 Author researched and created diagram and had it professionally digitally drawn on Fiverr.com

Set in motion by a perceived danger or fear, the Fight or Flight response triggers short-term thinking designed to help us safely extricate ourselves from life-or-death scenarios; nothing else matters.

What the Fight or Flight response reaction does is to put every aspect of your body into extreme focus. Ready to react at any chance or opportunity. No doubt a positive act in a dangerous situation. The downside is that when we are not in a real-life dangerous situation, it still is very limiting in its focus. The body doesn't view 10 or 100 or 1,000 options; just two. One thousand years ago this was exactly the recipe for survival, but in today's world, boiling your life down to two options is "fatal" in a different respect.

This survival instinct, at onset, is automatic and functions independently of your conscious control (in the short term, you do have the ability to fairly quickly regain full awareness). The quicker you can identify the survival instinct and, when applicable, acknowledge it is driven only by fear and not an actual danger, you can make the best conscious decision versus reacting.

Once the perceived threat has concluded, your body will return to its normal levels of hormones and physical functions. However, a key part of this is "once the threat has concluded" in modern life, all too often the "threat" is constant and never seems to "conclude." Stress at work, tight finances, family conflict, spousal disagreements, and so on : they all seem frightening in a way and the body thinks it is under constant attack. Therefore, the Fight or Flight response is constantly engaged and this leads to numerous unhealthy side effects.

 "...the fast pace of modern life seems to frequently trigger our fight-or-flight response," Dr. Sudha Seshadri, professor of Neurology [1]

There is great news for us in present life, as our brains have evolved over time, from one of managing basic bodily functions to higher logical thought. The human race has also increased cerebral control over these more basic functions by increasing reliance on the cerebral cortex. Meaning that when Fight or Flight sets in, we now have a more powerful tool to use: the cerebral cortex. To use this powerful part of our brain, we must give ourselves a cue to re-engage our logic state of mind.

Now that we are done with the science part, is important to recognize that at key times, adrenaline serves us very well. Here is a short first-hand story:

A few years ago, I remember my son was very young, and I was still learning my way through fatherhood. He was standing, but not quite walking yet. We were in the bathroom, somewhere between the bathtub and the toilet, and I was adjusting his diaper when he reached up and pulled down on the lid on the back of the toilet bowl. It was not on the toilet correctly and just by him pulling with his little body weight, it fell toward him.

I don't remember reacting, but the next thing I knew my left hand pinned the lid against the toilet water tank and my right arm was wrapped around him. The lid did fall far enough to hit the seat and crack but with no injury to anyone... all thanks to my adrenal gland! I reacted to the danger or bodily harm for my son; there was **no time to think**.

It is a powerful attribute and useful today, however, at the same time it doesn't serve you well in everyday life as it can be triggered by constant daily stressors or even stressors that are only in your own head and fears that are unlikely to play out. On the whole, most stressors today are intellectual, social, or professional in nature, and for these, adrenaline is far less useful.

"I've had a lot of worries in my life, most of which never happened." --Mark Twain

_____

1. Mckinney, Calum. (2019, January 18). Study Finds. Stress Can Literally Shrink Your Brain. www.studyfinds.org/stress-can-litterally-shrink-your-brain-study-finds/

THANKFUL, NOT THANKFUL TODAY

From an evolutionary point of view, I'm **thankful** for the Fight or Flight response in my life today, and thankful that my ancestors had it and used it when needed. For sure, there have been many key moments in my life when it has been invaluable.

Last time I needed it, I was on Interstate 35, sitting in a traffic jam. Slowly traffic started to open up and speeds climbed quite quickly. A driver put on his turn signal and pulled over into my lane, as I focused on the car moving over, and up ahead cars were slamming on their brakes. Luckily, I was driving a car with brake-warning lights and sound, and it was "screaming" at me to brake. My Fight or Flight reaction kicked in and was needed right away. I slammed on the brakes and stopped with just enough space to share (thankfully, so did the cars behind me).

At the same time, where I'm **not thankful** for Fight or Flight is in my dearest relationships, one of them being with my wife, my closest one today. It is easy to understand how unhelpful that is when we have verbal conflict. I can feel my pulse quicken, my voice shake, and my breath shorten. These are all classic Fight or Flight responses. There is no danger in the situation — no tigers, no bears—and yet my body readies for a powerful counter.

However, when I quickly stop and consider the situation from a calm position (before Fight or Flight fully takes over), I know that I don't want to Fight with my wife and I don't want to move into a Flight frame of mind either. I want us to find a common ground, and I want to continue working on building a trusting relationship. Therefore, as soon as I realize that my body starts getting ready to enter Fight or Flight state of mind, I consciously take back control; only at that point can I make the best decision for myself and my relationship.

This is interesting because even though I know that Fight or Flight has no place in this part of my life, it still manages to show up, and it will continue to be there every time a tense conversation starts or conflict arises. And the longer I allow Fight or Flight to stay in control of me physically and mentally, the more it can and will damage my relationship.

With this book, my greatest wish for you is that you learn to recognize when Fight or Flight shows up and how it is running your life, and as soon as you realize that, I hope that the next time you work on making the best different decision for you.

FIGHT OR FLIGHT! MAKE BETTER DECISIONS TO ENJOY YOUR LIFE QUICK WIN

Pay close attention when you feel stress building up in regards to a topic or even coming into contact with an individual. It is very possible that your Fight or Flight response has kicked in. Becoming aware of this state is an important first step. We can now start to do something different versus allowing the response to take over and the conflict to intensify.

FEAR VS. DANGER

WHAT IS FEAR AND WHAT IS DANGER?

Will Smith quoted in the movie After Earth:

 "Fear is not real. The only place that fear can exist is in our thoughts of the future. It is a product of our imagination, causing us to fear things that do not at present and may not exist. Do not misunderstand me danger is very real, but fear is a choice." [1]

The best place to start this awareness journey is to become clear on the difference between Fear and Danger. In other words, to clearly see the difference of when and where you are in a dangerous situation compared to when you're reacting out of fear in your life.

Everyone's lives are bombarded with fearful stories, mindsets, thoughts and actions. There can be more reasons to be fearful today than at any other time in our existence. We are more fearful for our children, our retirement, job security, possible divorce, addictions and so on.

Taking a step back we've now introduced a second situational factor. Fear can be found at any time in our lives or situation. The more we look for and allow fear into our life, the more it will be found. As simple as it sounds, it is true; we find what we are looking for in our life.

We live in a fear-ridden world, and if we chose to find a fearful thought or situation, it is not difficult to find it. Not too long ago we would watch daily newscast broadcasting stories of doom and gloom once or twice a day for 30 minutes. Nowadays this type of content is available whenever we pick up our phone or tablet. We can see breaking news anytime, or an email or a text message just coming in with the latest headline.

According to a Business Insider article by Antonio Villas-Boas, "The top concern is having personal and financial information hacked, which has 67% of those who were surveyed, worried."[2] The article continues to state that the top "conventional crime" which 3 percent of people worry about is having our car broken into or stolen. Amazingly, 6 percent worry about being assaulted or killed while at work. At this point we can start to dissect our concerns to better understand if they are within our control or not. Additionally, are we dealing (or will potentially have to deal) with a fearful or dangerous situation.

More so, we also have the ability to invent stories in our own head. It is very possible to raise your heart rate and breathing pace just by thinking of a past frightening situation, or an imaginary future situation, created in your brain. Don't get me wrong. Absolutely, there is danger in the world today, but as we live our daily lives, we must understand a key defining factor: is it truly a dangerous situation or I am feeling fearful and can choose to see the situation from a different angle?

This leads us into our next deeper step in Fear vs Danger.

My number one top fear is my cancer returning.

Fear Versus Danger

The Houston Chronicle published a list of top fears of Americans. When considered one by one, all would hold some level of discomfort for each of us.

The Houston Chronicle also published a list:

- Walking home at night alone
- Becoming Victim of ID Theft
- Safety of the Internet
- Mass Shooting
- Public Speaking

All of these fears put your body to work to protect you with your Fight or Flight mechanism. Once this old part of your brain fully kicks in to protect you, it takes over your entire body and any logical reasoning. At that advanced point, it greatly restricts your action and reaction options.

From a Fight or Flight point of view, let's perform a thought exercise and examine the previous list in more depth and identify the role of Fight or Flight. Some of these are legitimately **dangerous** instances where Fight or Flight is important and necessary.

Situation	Mental or Physical Threat	Fear or Danger Based Situation	Applicable use of Flight or Flight Response?	Fight or Flight Ruining or Enhancing Life?
Walking alone in a dangerous neighborhood	Physical	Dangerous	Absolutely	Enhancing
Victim of ID theft	Mental	Fear	Unlikely	Ruining
Safety on the internet	Mental	Fear	Unlikely	Ruining
Mass Shooting (Imaginative)	Mental	Fear	Unlikely	Ruining
Mass Shooting (Actual)	Physical	Dangerous	Absolutely	Enhancing
Public Speaking Opportunity	Mental	Fear	No	Ruining
Public Speaking Delivery	Mental	Fear	No	Ruining

This is how the change can be applied: Living in a state of fear, in this scenario, is the time an individual uses their mind to look into the future and see the possibility to be hurt, often without much of a possibility of it really happening. This imaginary hurt could be physical, mental, emotional, or financial. Meanwhile, the state of danger is an actual scenario when an individual must immediately act to ensure their (and their loved one's) physical safety.

Our adrenal glands were designed for life-threatening situations. When we are experiencing a dangerous situation, our adrenal glands are incredibly useful and necessary.

On the contrary, our adrenal glands were not designed to be used on a daily/hourly/minute-by-minute basis to deal with what we perceive as stressful situations and mentally created potential fear.

MENTALLY CREATED POTENTIAL FEARS

Our brains are great at collecting information and using past experiences and new information to look and plan into the future. The down side of this ability is that often, as years pass and as stories add new enlightenment, it is often thought we can see clearly into the future. This causes us problems because, based on past information, our brains and bodies start to anticipate how to react to potentially fearful situations. This turns on and increases our stress response and our Fight or Flight reaction.

It is important to note that these potential fears are valid for each individual. If they were not valid, we could just remove them from our world and minds and go on in a peaceful state. The challenge is that when we mix in our past with current fearful events and then project this state into our future, we can convince ourselves that all the perceived fears and dangers are valid. They rob us of an experience even before we have an opportunity to live it.

Once, I received a letter from the Internal Revenue Service (IRS)! I left it sitting on my kitchen counter for 4 days. I didn't touch it again after I brought it in. It was on my mind every moment. My pulse would quicken, my breath would shorten, and I'd have a sinking feeling in my stomach.

I lived in **potential fear** for 4 days of what was inside the envelope, and my mind created numerous horrible outcomes. For 4 days I lived in this state and I had no idea what was inside.

I opened it! I'd made a calculation error and owed $700. It wasn't great news, but the letter was hardly a good reason to use my Fight or Flight response. I was in no danger. I simply feared the words on a piece of paper, which I built up and exaggerated. (Note: I called the IRS, spoke with two agents who were incredibly helpful, and discussed the situation. Turns out it was a clerical error and I owed $0.)

Has anything similar happened to you, when you have used your Fight of Flight response for no good reason?

In summation, when your pulse starts to quicken, or when considering the reasons why you acted the way you did during a past event, decide if you viewed the situation as dangerous. Then decide if it is truly was dangerous, or fear had a hold of you. What are your biggest fears in life? What are your daily fearful thoughts? Are they a good use of your Fight or Flight response?

---

1. Producer Pinkett, C., Smith J., Smith, W., Lassiter, J., Shyamalan, M.& Director Shyamalan, M. (2013). *After Earth* [Motion Picture]. United States. Columbia Pictures.
2. Villas-Boas, Antonio. (November 10, 2017). Business Insider. Americans Far More Worried About Getting Hacked Thank Murder.
   https://www.businessinsider.com/americans-far-more-worried-about-getting-hacked-than-murdered-2017-11

ROBS LIFE OF OPPORTUNITIES

Fear and Danger are so close on the sensory spectrum that our brains cannot tell them apart in a split second.

While both can move us into a Fight or Flight frame of mind, one has the aspect of possible real fatality (danger), and the other one is the idea that something bad will or could happen (fear). However, in the very moment that Fear/Danger is upon us, the brain cannot distinguish between the two in the moment. Therefore, we need to train ourselves so that once our autonomic nervous system starts to run its course, we distinguish as soon as possible if we've moved into a state of Fear or physical Danger.

Again, if we are in danger, then Fight or Flight is the reaction we want in the moment to protect ourselves, and our adrenal glands and nervous system are the right tools for the job. However, if we've moved into a place of fear, then Fight or Flight is unlikely to be our best manner in which to approach the situation. Thankfully, in today's world the number of dangerous situations has decreased, but unfortunately the chance to see fearful situations has only multiplied.

Let's go through it together in an "unexpected event" that causes you to move to a state of fear or that danger is upon you, or even fear of what might happen. At the first opportunity we have to regain clarity from a shocking situation. We are well served to train our brains to think about our best option(s). This step is very important as at this point it puts us back in control, and our Fight or Flight response will fade. We can start to ensure that it will **not** run and ruin our lives. Understand that by defaulting to Fight or Flight when fearful, we rob ourselves of opportunities that will enhance our lives.

Choose to face the fear directly and go straight through it. The payoff over a lifetime is enormous.

In the very moment, determining whether the situation promotes a Fear vs Danger response might not be easy, but by observing and training ourselves we will soon have the ability to see it differently. It might be helpful the next time you need to decide how to best respond to a situation:

F False
E Evidence
A Appearing
R Real

Another meaning for Fear is the Opportunity to be Brave! And an opportunity to raise the heart rate and prove you're alive!

Choice is where it all begins. With choice a world of possibilities opens to you and your relationships. Choice is key.

Unfortunately, there is no choice in the Fight or Flight state of mind; it is only a survival reaction, and so choice allows you to make the best decision for you and your loved ones around you, and it gives you rational thought.

FIGHT OR FLIGHT! MAKE BETTER DECISIONS TO ENJOY YOUR LIFE QUICK WIN

It can be extremely beneficial to conduct a quick mental exercise before you're potentially engaged in the next Fight or Flight moment. Think about a fight from the past that is likely to repeat itself. Make a conscious decision if your mate would ever put you in danger. If the answer is yes, then take steps today to get yourself to a safe place.

If the answer is no…

Generally speaking, the answer is no; they would not put you into actual danger. In those cases, you must act accordingly when faced with such **fearful** situations. When you experience such a fear-based situation, then you have a better opportunity to move into a mental place of choice and rational thinking, so you can consciously avoid a Fight or Flight response. At the very least, if you go into Fight or Flight mode, you can move back into choice as quickly as possible. In this end state, you can do what is best for everyone involved.

The flip side is that if you don't consciously rule out danger and allow fear to take over your life, what will be the result of the conversation or situation? In the short and long run, it will not be positive or healthy for those engaged.

Thus. if you are not in danger and fear is something you can conquer and see as an opportunity… what do your **fears** cost you in life?

YOUR BIGGEST FEARS

Take a deep look at your biggest fears. I can tell you mine (Fear of Failure and Change) almost won.

As I graduated from high school, I made the choice to continue my studies on the college level. I applied to three schools and was rejected by my top choice Texas A&M. I appealed and was finally accepted on probation basis. If I didn't pass my first semester, then I'd immediately be expelled.

Fear of failure was staring me in the face. Everyone was watching, wondering how would I do in university. My friends all were off to school, my baby sister was on track to attend Texas A&M the year after me. Making the change from a small Texas high school to one of the largest universities in the U.S. was full of uncomfortable change. I was full of self-doubt and anxiety.

Then my first exam (Sociology), I studied as much and as well as I knew how. I attended every class and read all assigned reading. As I sat for the exam, I felt challenged but comfortable. The following week I received my grade and I was pretty sure my academic time was done. As plain as day, I can still see the numbers at the top of the page in red: 56.

All my fears came crashing in on me and I was sure I was done and would be heading home in a matter of months. Fears were in charge of my life for the

time being and I had no understanding of what was driving me.

What are your biggest fears? How do they play out in your life today? Have you given yourself the opportunity to face them or simply avoided them? As long as they are within you, they will be in control.

Here's a list to consider:

1. **Fear** of Failure
2. **Fear** of Change
3. **Fear** of Uncertainty
4. **Fear** of Being Judged (Fear of Rejection)

1. FEAR OF FAILURE

The fear of failure strikes everyone. It has big power that holds you back **before** you even attempt or start a project or experience. It is an empowering habit to make yourself mentally aware of the pros and cons of a situation or decision you're considering (this is living with choice). When you move to a "no, because I'll fail," then you've moved into a Fight or Flight mindset, an either/or mode, and that's right... you've failed before even starting! Without attempting, or discussing with someone you trust, or making a rational decision, you've allowed fear to win and stop you immediately.

Instead of viewing it as a fear that you can explore, and be in a place of choice, you can work through and examine any given situation, otherwise you give your control away. Then you've lost an opportunity in your life. A lost opportunity is a sad state of life and even sadder if allowed to build up over years.

I suggest we see the situation as it is: "I'm fearful of..." and then decide if the fear is valid and if it trumps the opportunity (danger will be avoided every time). There is power in owning a fearful frame of mind. No shame in acknowledging it, once again, by acknowledging it is fear. Now you can take your next best step.

Think about the last time an opportunity of attempting something new and different appeared in your life. Did you meet it with an open mind versus fear? There is a lifetime of difference meeting opportunity while wearing glasses of choice rather than fear and danger, and then unmistakably shut down.

I can share with you that I also go through this mental process. A quick example from my life is writing this book and others that I have in the works.

My first book took over three years to be done, from the moment the first draft was written until I sent it to an editor. No doubt fear of failure (and being judged) played a key role in my slow progress. I allowed the fear to hold me up at every step. It limited me asking for feedback on the manuscript that included a loved one thinking it was a horrible idea or bad writing. Allowing friends and family to even know that I'm writing a book meant that they can support me, but if I don't tell anyone, then I won't fail in front of them. Also not giving myself the proper time to focus and write could mean that if I don't finish, I can't fail. It was an endless game to limit my commitment, so that I would never reach the end and possibly not succeed.

 Allow yourself to consider choices and changes. As you choose to face your fear of Failure, you come

to realize that you have the abilities to accomplish what you want in life. It will happen only once you start.

2. FEAR OF CHANGE

The only constant in life is Change. Logically we all know more is coming. Change will always be part of life. Why we fear change is that change sets up the unknown. Of course, we cannot control the unknown. We don't live in a video game where we can decide the colors, shapes and challenges of life. We live in a world where everything is moving in a state of living and dying.

Do you recall a recent experience where abrupt change caught you by surprise? What was your reaction? Did you experience your Fight or Flight reaction? To fight back against change, Fight or Flight again is not your answer. It is fruitless. There will only be more to come. Look back again into your life, has change brought you more pain or more fulfillment?

If change has brought you more pain than fulfillment, then it is completely understandable where and why your fear arises. On some level you believe the next change will bring pain. If on the contrary, it has brought more fulfillment, then what is the reason you choose today about fear vs. excitement? Maybe one specific past painful event caused fear of change in your life. It is worth thinking about it and analyzing it. Use your inherent logic to make a decision about the current situation of change. When you allow past memories to control your current life and decisions, you will miss out on newness. Past painful change does not predict the future, so don't fear change.

Decide that you can deal with and heal past painful change and it can be of benefit to you from now on. You must understand it is in the past, not still happening to you in the now.

How long will you allow this type of fear to live in your life? Control your life? To decide what your future looks like? Change is coming, rejoice or you will continue to live in a fruitless Fight or Flight.

 Fears must be identified and brought to awareness in your life. Once you are made aware, their power over your decisions fade.

3. FEAR OF UNCERTAINTY

The fear of uncertainty is available to you around every corner, under every circumstance, and in everyone you meet on the street. When you focus your thinking on the different scenarios of uncertainty, they will lead you to see only that in this world. You can feel uncertain about your health, job, relationships, safety, financial security and so on. And sometimes, all it takes is to watch the nightly news. This mindset will creep up and take away your life—no exaggeration.

However, there is a paradoxical situation with living life; it's fulfillment and the involvement of uncertainty. When outcomes in life are certain, people tend to feel more comfortable and in control, and this sounds positive, but it is part of the paradox. Life doesn't remain certain for long and that is a good thing. When new things come and you are hit with uncertainty, it becomes a shock to the system and you feel uncomfortable and out of control… and again, that is a good thing.

 Truly living life means that life is uncertain; it is unnerving.

Choose to live life, accepting that life is uncertain and that is proof you are fully living life and not stuck. The opposite could quickly bring you to be the walking dead, which is alive on the outside and dead on the inside. Uncertainty can also mean excitement. Give yourself the gift of seeing uncertainty with new eyes, and on your last day you will see every chance you took as a success, especially the one big chance that led life into a new exciting direction.

Choose to see there are two sides to every situation and every story. For every moment of uncertainty, there are times of trust. Know and understand what is within your control and what is outside of your power. No one can know with complete certainty how a situation will end. You can trust in your ability to handle and deal with the situation as it appears.

There's one thing for sure: Uncertainty is certain in your life. Will you allow the fear of it to rob you of your joy for life, or will you focus where your dreams come true? Don't fear it.

 Once fear appears in your life, move towards it and challenge it, you'll find that the fear is not as powerful as it first appears.

4. FEAR OF BEING JUDGED

Whose opinion matters most in your life? Your family's? Your friends'? Yours? What about Joe and Jane Doe down the street or in the other department at work? Is that how you live your life? Do you allow the fear of being judged to hold you back from stepping out of your comfort zone?

Inside your comfort zone, you know what you'll get out of life, exactly what you have today. The exciting part—your dreams coming true—where you live in passion is outside that comfort zone in the unknown. With fear and no uncertainty, life gets smaller and more constrictive. Is that what you want from your life?

One thing you must know and keep in mind: Others will always judge you in life for what you do or don't do. They will judge you if and when you step outside your comfort zone, and they will judge you if you do not. Therefore, of what use is it to put much weight on their opinion? Focus on what you think of yourself and what your loved ones think of you. Others will get over it. Don't allow the appearance of judgment to stop you from doing what you know you want to do. The only person you have a right to judge is you today vs. who you were yesterday.

Fear of judgment sets up the opportunity for a Flight response. Instead of facing the potential for judgment, Flight moves in and takes over. In that place, you never allow yourself to get emotionally close to the person or persons (for fear of judgment). Instead you head for the closest exit and never look back. It costs you what you most want in your life—healthy and close relationships.

 What you want most in your life is on the other side of your fears. Once faced, fulfillment is abundant.

FEARS ALL AROUND YOU

In all these situations and fears already outlined, you must identify as quickly as possible if there is or is not an actual danger. If there is no danger to you, then go straight into your fear. There is only one way to face fear, and that is straight through it. Yes, you'll be stepping out into uncertainty and fear, but what is your other choice? If you choose to stay exactly where you are in life, it can be more damaging—living at less than you know you are capable, stuck in your comfort zone.

FIGHT OR FLIGHT! MAKE BETTER DECISIONS TO ENJOY YOUR LIFE QUICK WIN

A little trick I like to use is a question I ask myself when danger and fear show up in my life, and I've identified it as fear (not dangerous) and am in the process of making a logical decision about how I want to proceed: "What is the worst thing that can happen?" By engaging my conscious brain, it is not that fear magically goes away, it is actually still there, but I think about my worst-case scenario in a more realistic way. Most likely, it's not like I'm going to end up under a bridge dead. Typically, I'll find the potential upside much greater than the realistic down side. If I let fear get to me and take over, then in my mind I'll end up looking at the down side and worst possible case.

Fight or Flight does not have a place when facing a life opportunity. Fight or Flight, as a way of life, will give you only stress and fewer and fewer dreams coming true. Fear is a choice but danger is life threatening. Until you can see the difference, fear will ruin and run your life. Make it a choice.

One example in my life of how fear has robbed me of opportunities is that I always wanted to create a weekend program for men. I had the idea worked out on some simple overviews of the agenda, thought about how to promote it and with whom I'd like to work. Then I paused the process and put the idea on the shelf for over two years.

It kept eating at me to work on it further. Every time I shared the idea with people, I trusted they would be excited and I'd get a little further in the process. Next thing I knew it was many months later and nothing had been done.

Finally, a friend asked what was keeping me from moving forward, and his question forced me to take inventory. I was fearful. Fearful that no one would show up, that it would not be a success, and that people would judge me after it was finished. It was my first time dreaming a new program from scratch.

I found it very difficult to go beyond my fears, no matter how much my friends encouraged me to go forward. Until I stopped and identified the fears and made a conscious decision to not allow Fight or Flight to be in control, finally I'd stop allowing fear to control me and took my next best step into success. The worst thing that could happen was that I'd do nothing. I was the only one standing in the way of progress.

I pushed through the fears. Was I still fearful at times? Yes, and I did it anyway. Now six Choices Men's Weekend programs later, I feel successful and fears have subsided. My fear was in control until I allowed myself to take action.

PART 2: FIGHT OR FLIGHT AND OUR HEALTH

Mental and physical health are the most important possessions we have over our lifetime. If we exercise, we get stronger physically. If we eat well, we feel healthier. The same can be said of good mental health, in practicing what makes us stronger. Through my research and work in personal growth I'm clear that staying in a place of fear, of allowing Fight or Flight to be in control of our lives, is damaging to our health. To what degree is based on many factors. Such as, how long you live in the pressure state, pre-existing illnesses, how you take care of ourselves (mentally and physically) in your down time, and so on.

While the Fight or Flight's response is meant to keep us alive, today in many ways it impacts how well we feel in our day-to-day activities and beyond. We have examined in a big picture way how living in Fight or Flight impacts our lives, and in the following section we will go over its long-term impact in detail.

LONG TERM IMPACT OF LIVING IN FIGHT OR FLIGHT

HEALTH IMPACT—MIND & BODY

In the research for my book, I read studies and articles from: Washington Post, Houston Chronicle, Harvard Health, JAMA, books such as: Why Zebras Don't Get Ulcers and The Upside of Stress. My readings indicate that living in a constant state of Fight or Flight can play a role in exacerbating key mental health issues, such as an increase in the hormone production and sleep problems. Also, current research shows a negative impact for those who already have pre-existing mental health issues.

When you do just a little research or reading on the topic, you'll find the information is easy to obtain and the research is coming online quickly. Here is just a small sampling of what you might read further:

"Is Stress Making You Sicker?"[1] by Cedar-Sinai Staff (November 24, 2018)

"Stress! Don't Let It Make You Sick"[2] by Elizabeth Agnvall, AARP Bulletin (November 2014)

"Stress and Heart Health"[3] by American Heart Association (June 17, 2014)

Unfortunately, research at this point is not as clear-cut regarding the impact on mental health, and much more research is needed to fully understand its long-term impacts. But what is clear and widely known is that the mind and body are interconnected, and their relationship is incredibly complex. When minds constantly live in a space of fight and stress or flight and pessimism, humans stay in a constant state of alert, since it takes orders from the mind. This is draining for the mind and body. When the mind doesn't rest, then neither can the body. It is vital to turn off the mental stress and give your mind time to rest so the body can follow close behind.

An article from National Public Radio (NPR) under the title "High Stress Drives Up Your Risk of a Heart Attack describes the Mind / Body" link perfectly. The author, Allison Aubrey, states "...those who perceive a lot of stress in their lives are at higher risk of heart attacks and other cardiovascular problems over the long term." Long term can be identified as in months and years. Very important here is a key word in this statement is "perceive." It all starts in the mind, the way people see their daily stressors. The fear starts there, as does the act of getting the Fight or Flight response under control

A regrettable truth is that there are many situations and key moments in humans' lives when they can feel fearful for both short and extended periods of time. Therefore, they can practically be ready for having an "attack" just from individuals or situations. Maybe their spouse is unkind or edgy, their boss is angry, their child is unruly, and so on. And when individuals believe these scenarios are the norm in life, their minds are on guard to fight back and defend.

While one or more of these situations might be true in your life, by living in a constant state of stress, it damages your mental health and well-being. Let's work together so you can choose something better.

Now that you have identified some stressors that might have you living in a place of defending yourself, how likely is it that you'll take a prolonged view of mental health? Will you take the time to meditate? Will you look for ways to relieve a stressful mind? Thinking and decision making, from a temporary point of view, limits your options to obtain the healing and health you need in the now and lifelong view. Mental and physical health takes focus and commitment; it does improve well-being in the now, and most important there is a lasting impact. Unfortunately, people stop acting on the beneficial options for their mental health today, due to focus on the moment.

Some possible outcomes after living in a state of Fight or Flight for too long that will impact your mental health are:

- Increased Anxiety
- Agitation
- Sleep Disruption
- Irritability
- Quicker to Anger
- Suppressed Immune Response
- Chronic Headaches
- Panic Attacks

Leaving these impacts on their own, unattended for a short period of time, they are manageable. However, over an extended period of time they compound and impair the mental and physical body, and put added pressure on all relationships and any social interactions.

This way of living really creates a type of downward spiraling whirlpool. The habit of living in Fight or Flight leads to stressed relationships, body discomfort, and back to more Fight or Flight situations that negatively impact mental health … and then we start again, but in a greater degree.

I'm very clear about my situation when I've spent too much time in a state of Fight or Flight. Can you tell when you are at that moment?

The last time I can remember it impacting me from a mental point of view happened over a two-week period of time, in which I had a lot going on in my professional and personal life.

I found myself standing in a hotel parking lot feeling beyond agitated. I had a crick in my neck from the previous (short and restless) night's sleep. I was staring at my phone and ignoring the question coming at me from my co-worker. My blood pressure was rising and I had a pocket full of tissue to address my runny nose and was looking for some type of aspirin to address my headache (now on day 3).

It is a bit odd looking back, because it is so obvious now that I was using my Fight or Flight response to push me through those two weeks. At some moments it might have felt like I was taking on the world! I had just traveled internationally across North America, received a new big project that I was looking forward to taking on, and I'd recently received the news I'd be a father for a second time. At the time I was also looking for a new venue for our business and had met with multiple important clients, and my wife had decided to take time off work to be with our family.

Clearly, my body was exhausted from living on the edge of Fight or Flight. I'd used adrenaline too often and was paying the price, as were those around me. I was short with people who wanted the best for me, and exhausted, but not sleeping enough. As soon as my eyes would open (no matter the time), my brain was going full speed ahead. I had stress headaches and my body and immune system were telling me for days to slow down even while I pushed forward.

The downward spiral was in full speed ahead and I was only adding to it. I caused more tension for my wife, was not as attentive with clients, as well as missing important details and wasting time in business meetings. Then it came into focus as I stood there in the parking lot. I needed to take a deep breath and decide what was really important in that moment and carry out my next best decision. Was I in real danger? No, not really.

I took a few hours of calm, I stopped putting items on my calendar and to-do list and I categorized where I needed to focus versus making everything my focus. I slept. The next morning, in my rested state, I received numerous benefits. My headache was gone, my nose had stopped running, my anxiety calmed and my shortness with those around me lightened so that I could enjoy their presence. Our bodies are wonderful and responsive to our care.

I'd done it to myself (again) and impacted my mental state by living in Fight or Flight for too long. Though two weeks isn't long enough to have a permanent impact on health (I hope), it's certainly long enough to have a dramatic short-term impact. And to think, many people live in this fight-or-flight state for years—even decades. If this is you, we can stop this together.

At this point you can all clearly get out of that the Fight or Flight response that prepares every area of your body to give its maximum output. It readies your lungs, heart, brain, digestive tract to prepare for a life or death encounter. Fine for a moment of danger, but damaging when the stress perceived as fear lasts for months, years, over a career or marriage.

This chronic state of Fight or Flight, over time, leads to unhealthy impacts on the body. Some of the side effects related to this can be: digestive issues, headaches, sleep problems, as well as being hard on your heart and cardiovascular systems, plus increased risk of auto-immune disease.

Another interesting ramification comes when living life in a more pessimistic way, meaning that you tend to always expect the worst in life and thus have your body on stand-by (like the boxer in the ring, in beginning of the book) for a Fight or Flight situation. If that's the case, these are some side effects you'll be looking at:

- Higher Blood Pressure
- Weakened Immune System
- Increased Chance of a Heart-Attack
- Increased Chance of a Stroke
- Cardiovascular System Stresses

Additionally, pessimistic individuals are more likely to have poor cardiovascular health and are less likely to take care of their body and health (less likely to exercise and eat well). Most likely the decision made here will be with short-term thinking, therefore making poor decisions for the long term by focusing only on "today." However, please note that it is not by living in a state of optimism that automatically makes your cardiovascular system healthier, but it is one life factor that manifests itself in our motivations regarding lifestyle decisions.

Putting these two last points together makes it definitely worth keeping an eye on our thoughts. Clear the mind, focus on the positive and what you want to experience in life. Let's expect the best is yet to come, since you know focusing on fear and danger will push away health and your dreams and passions in life.

The long-term impact on our bodies is profound. We must start in our minds so we can limit the negative impact on our body. We must take care of our mental experiences to regain control of our adrenal glands. Always keep in mind that our bodies will go where our minds lead it.

While I was researching for this book, I came across an article that quickly became one of my favorites. It is titled "Watching an Eagles Game is Literally a Workout, Doctors Say"[4] by Stephanie Stahl. It's a caution from doctors for men watching an NFL playoff game! The take-away for us is in some cases, for individuals with severe heart conditions, becoming over-excited can be dangerous. This is probably not a surprising statement, however linking it to watching a football game is interesting. Dr. Susan Fidler of Abington Family Medicine, quoted in this article, continues to say "...for the rest of us, get ready for a hormone overload...your heart rate and blood pressure response can be that of high exertion exercise."

This is a perfect example of how in your ordinary life, people allow or incite Fight or Flight, and how it could potentially impact your health. Humans are surrounded by an unlimited amount of opportunities to live in Fight or Flight and impact their bodies.

Can you think about any in your life?

There is a wide range of how a daily state of Fight or Flight can lead you to damaging your body. None of the options are where you want to live your life over the years ahead. The daily adrenaline-filled state does not serve you well. You can better your health today and improve your health of tomorrow by learning to keep your Fight or Flight response in check.

---

1. Cedars Sinai. (2018, November 24)."Is Stress Making You Sicker?" www.cedars-sinai.org/blog/is-stress-making-you-sicker.html
2. Agnvall, Elizabeth. (2014 November). AARP. "Stress! Don't Let it Make You Sick" www.aarp.org/health/healthy-living/info-2014/stress-and-disease.html
3. American Heart Association. (2014, June 17). "Stress and Heart Health" www.heart.org/en/healthy-living/healthy-lifestyle/stress-management/stress-and-heart-health
4. Sahl, Stephanie. (2019, January 11). CBS Local Philadelphia. "Watching An Eagles Game is Literally A Workout, Doctors Say." https://philadelphia.cbslocal.com/2019/01/11/watching-an-eagles-game-is-literally-a-workout-doctors-say/

HEALTH IMPACT—YOUR CHILDREN

This section is where the book idea began. I read the Newsweek article "This is Your Brain on Poverty"[1] as I wanted to know how I could be a better father for my young son. It was eye-opening for me to understand how big a role stress had on my life and then on that of my son's. I further researched stress and how it is brought into our lives and what we can and can't control, which lead me to researching our Fight or Flight response and this book.

In my experience, no area is more difficult to write and talk about than how our stress might and does impact a child. At this point, it is easy to acknowledge that too much and too long an exposure to Fight or Flight situations is not healthy. From that point forward, it becomes very complex and difficult to draw specific conclusions on how it will impact a child's life. So, now you are moving past yourself and into the people you love the most on this earth. My position as a parent circles back to the beginning: how I deal with Fight or Flight in my life will impact my son.

By his observations of how safe I feel (at home, in the street, in our surroundings, and so on), it directly impacts how he will experience his environment. Also, how I deal with these situations is a likely indicator how he will also handle such occurrences in his own life. If I continually rely on my Fight or Flight response in life, it is unlikely he will have a healthy view of fear.

While it is understandable to be on edge in a difficult life situation, when that situation becomes a constant in life and is passed on our children, they are forced to live it out over their key developmental years and their mind/brain is greatly impacted.

There is further evidence that points to the life-long impact of stress on a child. For example, according to the book *The Upside of Stress* by PhD Kelly McGonigal,[2] psychologist, author of groundbreaking research, and educator, "...your early experiences with stress can have a strong effect." She continues with "Adults who experienced abuse during childhood...are more likely to have learned not to trust others in stressful times." They learn that people are not trustworthy and therefore are more likely to rely on their Fight or Flight response when they come into new situations and meet new acquaintances.

While none of this can predict how a child will ultimately live their life or the decisions they'll make in 10 or 20 years, it is important to understand that putting a young brain in constant or extreme Fight or Flight situations does change their brain development, point of view, and how they deal with the world.

As a parent, one must understand and do their part to not allow fear to lead them in life and to make short-sighted decisions. It is my work as a parent to do that. I cannot expect him to do anything different than what I'm showing him.

A child should never be exposed to abuse, lack of safety, addictions, lack of stability, extreme fighting, and having no emotional or physical attention. These, and more, are within your control as a parent, so you must stop and limit them. All have the potential to impact children so they become hypersensitive to any threat or potential threat that could move them into a quicker Fight or Flight response.

Remember how at the beginning of the book I asked you to see yourself as the boxer? Now, I want you to envision your child as the untrained boxer; they are more quickly prepared to move into a place of Fight or Flight to save their life (emotional or physical) versus living like a professional boxer who can see the threat coming and decide how to respond.

Still today, I am famous in my family for asking (and sneaking a peek) if we have enough gas in the vehicle (car or boat). Let me tell you why. When I was five years old, I experienced two events that impacted the way I experienced life.

> One, when I was that age, we went to my grandmother's lake cabin on Possum Kingdom Lake in North Texas. I don't remember the beginning of the boat trip around the lake, but I do remember when the boat stopped in the middle of the lake. I was filled with fear as my grandmother and mother attempted to understand why it stopped and didn't restart. It was due to a faulty fuel gauge. I fed off their stress of having two young children in a trying situation. With no one else around, my mom jumped in the water and swam, pulling the boat to shore. From the five-year-old's point of view that was an incredibly dangerous situation—absolutely life or death!

That same year in Midland, Texas, as we went down the street, our car ran out of gas! The short version of this story is that my mom ended up pushing the little convertible to the side of the road and then we walked home.

From that year forward, and for many years to come, I have been famous for asking every time my mom and grandmother when we got in the boat or car, "Do we have enough gas?" and "What will happen if we run out of gas?" Those were probably the closest to death (extreme exaggeration) I'd experienced in my young life. It greatly impacted me.

As I grew older, one could imagine I should have gotten over it. However, it carried on through my adolescence and teen life. I can honestly remember watching TV and worrying that Bo and Luke Duke would run out of gas as they raced away from the sheriff on the show The Dukes of Hazzard!

We truly never know how a traumatic (or just inconvenient) event will impact the child. I'm positive it was not traumatic to my caregivers. However, two inconveniences (from the adult perspective) impacted me for years.

I am not saying that kids are never to experience real life events, which sometimes are very inconvenient, but this is just an example of how something ordinary created stress in me and marked the way I saw a simple thing like having enough gasoline. Therefore, we can only imagine the impact of a real stressful situation and its constant repetition. Moreover, how the parent handles, the kid handles and will handle. How might a legitimate dangerous situation, faced by a child, play out over their lifetime? I am hoping is in your hands to help out.

Children may grow to look for threats in every situation and experience. Which brings us back to the long-term impact it may carry for them mentally and physically. I believe these types of traumas experienced in childhood will impact our entire life. The child is defenseless and needs their caregivers in order to survive. When our Fight or Flight response is repeatedly enacted, demonstrated, and experienced as successful (the parent and child survived), then the child will know that tool will work and be likely to do as the parent and rely on it in the future.

Under my control, as a parent, I'm responsible, from birth onward, for the amount of stress I allow into my life and how I deal with that stress in my daily activities. My child is not responsible, but children are exposed to it at a young age through many factors of their environment and by observing their parents.

When the time comes that my children see me, indeed, facing a dangerous situation, they will be frightened too. Their Fight or Flight response will kick in too. They will look to me to protect them.

As parents, we will always do our best and is important to do our best in what happens next... how I handle the post-situation actions and lessons. Do I "get back on the horse" and continue on, or do I stay in a stressed state for a prolonged period of time? Do I move into fear with similar situations?

All of this is in my control, and my son is watching everything I do and learning how he should respond in the moment and in the aftermath. Remember, children are the most perfect observers, however, they are poor interpreters of the complexity of adult situations.

CHILDREN ARE WONDERFUL OBSERVERS AND POOR INTERPRETERS.

How many times have you seen a child fall down? One of their first reactions is to turn their focus to the parent. They are looking for feedback from the parent "Am I going to be ok?" or "Is this supposed to be scary?" and "Should I cry or just keep on walking?" They will react largely based on your reaction.

If the parent moves into fear, so will the child. If the parent choses to move into logical thought to dissect the situation, then a Fight or Flight lesson can be passed along from parent to child.

My desire for you as parents, aunts, uncles, grandparents and mentors is to gain understanding of your Flight or Flight response. Know when it not a good idea to rely on it in life and how to deal with it as soon as possible after you've entered such a state. My children and your children's physical and mental health will be impacted based on how we handle Fight or Flight on a daily basis.

Furthermore, if you were that child who faced a horrible situation growing up, it can be curative to you, as an adult, to bring healing to your past. It will allow you to move out of, or lessen the impact, that Fight or Flight has in your life today.

FIGHT OR FLIGHT! MAKE BETTER DECISIONS TO ENJOY YOUR LIFE QUICK WIN:

When your child is facing a fearful situation, verbally lead them through the process of relaxing their body and making the best decision they can in the moment. Your leadership and teaching will pay off huge in their life.

1. Hayasaki, Erika. (2016, August 25). Newsweek Magazine. "How Poverty Affects the Brain" https://www.newsweek.com/2016/09/02/how-poverty-affects-brains-493239.html
2. McGonigal, Kelly Ph.D., *The Upside of Stress: Why Stress is Good for You, and How to Get Good at It*, Reprint edition, Avery, 2016. https://www.penguinrandomhouse.com/books/316675/the-upside-of-stress-by-kelly-mcgonigal/

DIFFERING IMPACT OF
ADRENALINE

While Fight or Flight are the two best known reactions to dangerous situations, there are other reactions that are associated with a rush of adrenaline. Such as, Freeze, Fawn, Fib, or Tend and Befriend. It is not as straightforward as Fight or Flight. However, the point holds that none of these reactions are the most healthy manner to deal with the situation.

For example, I find this fascinating that in the animal kingdom, the Freeze reflex is part of the adrenaline response. The most famous example here in Texas is the possum. The possum will play dead when it is faced with a dangerous situation. I remember clearly finding one in our trash can as a young boy. My father and I opened the can and it didn't move. I could not even see it breathing. My father assured me it was well and alive. We laid the trash can down on the ground and stepped back. Within a minute, it took off for the tree line as fast as it could.

The Freeze reflex is also applicable to humans. You may have encountered it when faced with a threat or unexpected irrational individual. Maybe the threat was not directed at you, but you were in the area. The Freeze reaction is used to keep the "predator" from noticing you and/or keep the predator's kill instinct from taking over. This could save you in a life-threatening situation.

As adults in a fearful situation, but not in a life-threatening situation, the Freeze reaction does not work to build relationship, to establish trust, or demonstrate leadership skills.

During stressful, but not threatening times, the Fawn reaction (to court favor, be extremely nice, show excessive respect), might look like someone using over-the-top flattering words and phrases toward another individual who's acting in a confrontational manner. This may be seen in individuals who've had an unhealthy upbringing. They are quick to give compliments in a stress-filled situation. It may have been learned as a type of survival mechanism in their youth, as a coping mechanism to avoid a fearful situation.

As adults in a fearful situation, the Fawn reaction does not work to build deeper relationships and it puts them in a place of always giving and never receiving.

Concerning the Fib response, think about a young child who's put into a situation of being asked by an irritated parent, "What happened?" They are fearful of the punishment or parent. Therefore, instead of taking accountability for the issue, they choose to Fib. As we know, this doesn't work out well for the child. When this response is carried into adulthood and used in fearful situations, then trust is lost after repeated Fibs; it doesn't work.

Finally, Tend and Befriend in a dangerous situation can have great advantages for protection. In a fearful situation, it can convolute relationships and interactions and make the primary relationship more unstable. The individual may confide in friends about the last fight or issues in the relationship (which can be a healthy action); however; if they never return and work on the issues in the primary relationship, then there is little hope for improvement and increased safety and trust.

Tend and Befriend looks beneficial from the outside, it doesn't work for the long- term relationship. The core issues must be addressed and healed or they are left stuck in the loop of relationship conflict: Tend and Befriend, return to relationship, relapse of conflict, Tend and Befriend, and so on. Nothing is improved, the relationship is not growing and there is likelihood of repeating the situational conflict over and over.

I caution you, that just because one Fight or Flight reaction type might seem healthier than the others, they are all damaging over the long term to the relationship and home. A home and relationship need a safe and trusting place in order to thrive and become more. When there is either constant feeling of Fight/Flight or unhealthy nurturing (i.e., Fawn or Tend and Befriend) in the home, it will not be a healthy environment. Over time the foundation of the relationship will erode and the home will crumble. We must use our logical minds to create a growth-oriented mindset for ourselves and our loved ones.

ANGER DOES NOT LIVE IN
ISOLATION

One additional impact that adrenaline has on our lives is through the expression of anger. Anger is simply a technique we use to keep us safe when we are fearful. Without underlying fear, there is no anger.

FIGHT OR FLIGHT! MAKE BETTER DECISIONS TO ENJOY YOUR LIFE QUICK WIN

When anger appears in your life, ask, What is the true reason I'm fearful in this situation? Your response will provide key information to begin to deal with the root cause of the issue.

I have a story of a little red car that will help illustrate this perfectly. It was a toy car my son sat atop when he was under two years old. The more I thought about the story, the more I had adrenaline running through my body, and the more my anger grew. Now I understand that anger is intertwined with Fight or Flight and is linked back to Fear, and I am going to tell you why.

> My son was under two years old and had received a car that he could sit on and push himself around the house. He loved it. The car had a horn that made all kinds of fun sounds. He fell off the car quite hard one day and hit his head. He was fine but I was a bit worried. My wife and I spoke about how we could keep him safe while using it and implemented a few steps. Two days later when I

was with him alone, I turned when I heard him hit the ground and smack his head on the floor. I was so angry!

I grabbed him to make sure there was no damage to his little body, and as he cried, I felt my anger grow at that stupid car. He regained some composure, I put him down and picked up the car and opened the back door. I threw the car as far as I could and there it sat all day.

I told my wife we'd have to get rid of the toy car and, of course, she understood. She asked where it was and I told her I threw it out the back door. She mentioned that might not have been the best lesson to teach our son—to react with anger.

I thought it through and realized it wasn't the best lesson, but then I turned the question inward. Why did I have such a swelling of anger inside of me? I was in no way angry at my son. It did no good to be angry at the car. The best question I could ask myself was not about anger but fear. I had a huge amount of fear concerning my little son and not wanting him to be hurt. I had a huge amount of confirmed fear that I'd made a mistake and had not removed the toy the day before.

WHAT WE FEAR DRIVES OUR ANGER.

Anger is a strong emotion that many individuals use to create space between themselves and others. It works physically and emotionally, for people you've just met or long-term relationships, on the highway and in the home. It is a challenging emotion to relate to and understand. Individuals' use of anger can be instantaneous or built over years to a mighty explosion.

Anger comes about internally when people feel threatened—they feel a need to defend something. Rarely is anger a primary emotion. Frequently, there is an underlying emotion that is touched first. More often than not, fear is at the root of the anger outburst. To say it another way, specifically in regards to this book, Anger is the Fight part of Fight or Flight. When Fight or Flight is triggered, and Flight is not an option, then watch out for an angry individual.

As already discussed, without a life or death situation, it comes back to a fear-based creation in the mind. Hence, you're back to fear as the root of the Fight and/or Anger which is encountered.

To further complicate the emotional situation, society teaches us not show our weaknesses, as they will be used against us, and that they are not our pretty side. We're also taught to ignore our fears and focus on positives. All the while our fears and weaknesses are kept hidden, rarely expressed below the surface. But when they are touched in a moment in life when we are truly fearful and don't know how to deal with the situation, then we quickly move into Fight or Flight.

When you chose to fight, which in today's world an actual use of physical force is less likely, you move to your next best option, which is anger. You might use words, volume, tone, facial expressions, and your physical body to make your best attempt and get what you want. Your anger is turned outward while the root cause of the anger is inward.

Choosing to address and deal with weaknesses and fears can bring a healthier life. You become more and more vulnerable and open about what is at the root, then more emotionally honest. And that my friends, is freedom. However, in many ways your choice comes down to either 1) Act out in Anger or 2) Speak openly about your fears and be vulnerable.

I believe we can agree that our first reaction is typically choice 1. Shall we change that for our own health? If not, for our children's health?

Once you step into openness and vulnerability, your fear is then out in the open and anger is much more manageable. When any of these adrenaline "responses" is understood and recognized, then and only then can you stop the response from controlling the situation.

FIGHT OR FLIGHT! MAKE BETTER DECISIONS TO ENJOY YOUR LIFE QUICK WIN

Start by identifying your favorite response to adrenaline and when you realize that you're in the middle of the response, simply do something different in a healthy manner.

DO SOMETHING DIFFERENT IN A HEALTHY MANNER.

PART 3: FIGHT OR FLIGHT IMPACT ON YOU

POSITIVELY IMPACTS YOU TODAY: THREATS, SPORTS, REACTION TIME

At no point hear me saying that there is absolutely no place for Fight or Flight. At times (and I hope not too many), it will save your life or help you move positively forward. If you face an aggressive dog in the street, it is useful. While playing sports, there is always a shot of adrenaline to increase your physical preparedness, so it is useful. When driving on packed interstate highways at high speeds and having to stop quickly, it will be useful. At times we need our adrenaline glands to take over in a split second.

For a family member it absolutely saved his life a few years ago. Here is the story:

Some members of my family have owned an antique store on a small Texas back road to Wimberley. At that time, they'd been in business over ten years very quietly and peacefully. It was a normal Fall afternoon and my uncle was stripping furniture in the back shop, preparing it for the showroom floor to sell. As was common, he heard a random car pull into the drive. This was completely the norm as passersby would commonly stop at all hours of the day, any day of the week. My uncle glanced around the corner to see if the car was stopping or going to pull on through. In fact, it did stop and a large man emerged.

My uncle approached the car and asked how he could help, and the large man asked to see a few pieces of furniture that were for sale. My uncle was more than happy to show him what was available. They headed to the showroom, just the two of them, and looked at half a dozen pieces, then there was a strange sound (a bit of fear went off inside my uncle), and he turned to see what the large man was doing.

At that moment the large man pulled a knife and came down, aimed at my uncle. Luckily his adrenal gland was in full effect, and he threw up his arm and somewhat blocked and deflected the blade. Then with the full strength and instinct of his body, instead of fighting, he chose to flee in a millisecond. It saved his life.

No doubt Fight or Flight played a key role in his survival that day. No doubt it was invaluable for him to use every resource his body had to make it to safety.

On the other hand, there are those who choose to truly live life, those who are pushing the limits, knowing it will kick off their Fight or Flight response repeatedly in life (such as; extreme sport athletes, emergency room doctors, firefighters, etc.). Those who choose to push the limits are living a passion-filled life. You have these people in your life, they will start a conversation with anyone or will start a new business venture when last one failed. I personally seek out these type of individuals and befriend them. It pushes me in my life to live more fully.

The key, and the difference, in these two scenarios is to not let our Fight or Flight response keep us from living our passions, nor keep us from continuing to live that life of living in fear and later of regret. The most important point for all is to limit the influence that Fight or Flight has on our daily life and our decision-making process. Our beliefs will lead our thoughts, our thoughts will lead our actions, our actions will lead our days, our days will lead our lives. Start now and examine your beliefs about your fears. The payoff is a beautiful life.

RUINS YOUR LIFE TODAY

Generally speaking, the Fight or Flight response does not serve well when leading your families and children. Fight or Flight nor does not work well in your friendships. Neither does it assist in your professional lives.

When you bring children into this world, or as children enter your lives through extended family or marriage, you want the best for them. What that may look like is for them to live life to the fullest, to accomplish their dreams, have passion and close relationships. They learn all of this by watching their parents and close adult relationships in their life. If Fight or Flight is demonstrated on a frequent bases, that is the exact manner in which they will pattern their life.

Additionally, as you are hired for a job or take on new responsibilities at work, what do you believe your superiors and co-workers want to see from you and your work habits? Do you want to demonstrate lack of decision-making abilities, insecurity of direction, lack of self-compassion? Coworkers and superiors want you to succeed in the work place; as you become better and more, so do they.

If you believe it does serve you in any of these relationships, then dissect what is important to you and what you want to experience in your relationships. You'll likely find that the:

FIGHT OR FLIGHT RESPONSE DOES NOT HELP YOU IN OBTAINING WHAT YOU TRULY DESIRE FOR YOUR LOVED ONES.

For the most part, it does not serve you well. The most damaging place Fight or Flight robs you of connection, of making the best decision, or of having the most fulfilling life possible in your closest personal relationships with the people you love.

Think back for a moment into the beginning of an important primary relationship (past or current) with a significant other. What was the reason you entered that relationship? What were the hopes and dreams for yourself and the other individual? How much joy did that person bring into your life? When the relationship lives in a state of Fight or Flight, it defaults to two quasi-constant states: constant **fighting** (same topics, same discussion, same words, same unsuccessful outcome) or constant emotional and possibly physical **withdrawal** from the relationship. This is not the relationship of which you dreamed when you made the commitment, is that right?

Unfortunately, there is no healing function within the Fight or Flight response. So once again, you need to step back and take control of yourself.

The main reason it impedes many flourishing opportunities in all of our relationships is that it is good at its job. Therefore, the Fight or Flight reaction doesn't care if the threat is deadly or dangerous or risky. It doesn't care if you have a lack of confidence or a gamble or even a verbal "hit." It views all (potential and actual, real or imaginary) pain (mental, emotional and/or physical) as a threat to survival. It goes way overboard in the reaction. Ultimately, it eats away the foundations of all relationships, which is trust and safety. Without the establishment or reestablishment of these two states, the relationship will become hollow and dreams will die.

Some of the manners in which Fight or Flight impacts our lives and relationships are:

- Robs of Opportunities
- Either/Or Thinking Creates a Relationships Stuck in Conflict (Fight)
- Creates a Relationships which Lacks Intimacy (Flight)
- Keeps Relationships Stuck

The above list limits relationships by restricting the possibility of future positive outcomes. It also decreases growth and increased depth in conversations, ideas and attachment. In this state, couples often move to a place where they hold themselves back from taking a chance at something new and from taking calculated risks (such as, writing love letters, spending time alone with partners, and broaching topics where disagreement is possible). All too often, couples stop saying loving words to each other or they stop taking steps to accomplish a dream together or stop doing what is right for both in a conflictive situation.

Once the habit of Fight or Flight is set within any relationship, you can take any normal daily situation or interaction and create a fearful worst-case scenario. Once the mindset is created and believed to be true, it holds you back. Don't allow that scenario to determine your decision. Is it likely to happen? Not really. Then why would it lead your future?

Something helpful could be to balance out the worst-case and best-case outcome. In many ways it is easy to focus on the worst-case outcome as we are risk averse. By thinking of the best-case, we are engaging the logical brain and looking for additional outcomes. For example, faced with a job loss or company lay-offs. Fear will enter your mind; fear of losing your job, fear of losing your social network, fear of losing the house or maybe even not having food for the table. To bring a balanced perspective, conduct the mental exercise of best-case scenario. It is time for a new beginning, you know exactly what you want in a place of work, and now it is time to find it. You will learn a new skill set, and past mistakes you've made can now be utilized to grow and meet challenges.

Every opportunity passed is a lost opportunity to experience the best possible outcome and leaves you stuck right where you are. Remember that, at any given moment, you are building or destroying your relationship. If you are with the right person or someone you love deeply, choose wisely how to proceed.

> My son is four years old. For the past two years, I've asked him how I can be a better father. To date he hasn't answered me yet. Honestly, I'm incredibly nervous and fearful about the first time he looks me in the eye and says, "Dad you could be a better father by..."
>
> However, my fear doesn't stop me from asking. If I allowed that fear —the worst- case scenario—to run my life, it would rob me of a closer relationship with my son. I'm going to keep asking because I want to do my part for the best- case scenario in my life.

When we move from a place of logic, using our extremely powerful minds for reason, into a place of pure innate reaction, then it robs us of enjoying situations, relationships and our life pleasures.

How many loving opportunities have been lost due to your brain going to the worst-case scenario? How many times has fear taken over right before you move into a mindset of enjoyment.

FIGHT OR FLIGHT! MAKE BETTER DECISIONS TO ENJOY YOUR LIFE QUICK WIN

Ask those around you the hard questions, "How can I be a better mother/father/spouse/sibling?" Then sit in silence and focus on what the other person is communicating and don't move into Fight or Flight. This type of information is golden.

EITHER/OR THINKING

A DEEP DIVE

To talk about Either/Or Thinking, consider a challenging relationship at work or a topic you have with your partner that seems as though it can't be resolved, no matter the number of times it's been discussed. One of the most self-limiting actions is to enter a mindset of two options... Either this Or that. A two option (Either/Or) is the default mind set of Fight or Flight. When you find yourself in an emotionally fearful position, your mind moves into a focused set and seeks the fastest manner to "escape." We call this Either/Or thinking; either I do X or Y.

One or the other, X or Y, Fight or Flight, options are all you can see when adrenaline is flowing. It will produce results for you, but it is guaranteed that this method will not bring you the best outcome. The truth is, there are an unlimited number of options, by limiting yourself, the relationship will grind to a halt.

FIGHT

What are you to never speak about at dinner parties in the U.S.? Politics and Religion. What is the reason? It is that individuals tend to have very strong opinions about these two areas, and even the slightest variation in opinion will likely lead an intense debate (i.e., Verbal Fight). Once a verbal Fight begins, the brain quickly moves into Either/Or thinking:

FIGHT - EITHER/OR POSSIBLE EXAMPLES

Either	Or
I win this fight	I fear I'll look weak
I prove I'm right	I fear I'll look stupid, like a doormat
I yell louder so they hear my opinion	I fear I won't be heard

Does this look familiar? Have you found yourself on one side or the other before?

What is the error with moving into Either/Or thinking? From a survival point of view, it may offer a simple stand to make a decision (two choices) and therefore make it quick to act. This is a strength when one is faced with a dangerous life or death situation. "I'm ready to fight it out to protect myself or my family." However, moving into an Either/Or frame of mind, when you're not in danger, severely limits your options and gives you two **extreme** choices.

Let's return to the example of an intense discussion at a dinner party. At this party with friends and loved ones, you enter into a conversation about the next political election. Your best friend strongly disagrees with your point of view about who to support. Your brain feels as though you are under attack. When your best friend says "that is the stupidest thing I've ever heard" (a verbal hit), your brain releases chemicals and the adrenal gland goes to work. Ouch, that was painful... but why exactly is a verbal hit painful?

According to Matthew Leiberman, Professor and Social Cognitive Neuroscience Lab Director at UCLA Department of Psychology, Psychiatry and Biobehavioral Sciences, using neural imagining studies demonstrates that a social and physical pain have the same underlying neurological reaction in the brain. To state it another way, if you were to break an arm, your brain will light up on the brain scans (Functional Magnetic Resonance Imaging) the same as when you lose a loved one. What is the reason for this? We are social beings. Not long ago our very own survival was dependent on our group. Therefore, to be socially exiled by peers or family would be dangerous for an individual's survival. In his TED Talk about this topic, Lieberman calls the social pain just as important as the neurological pain of the broken arm or leg.[1]

Therefore, a verbal fight has the same reaction as a physical fight in the brain. This leads you to understand and confirm why the Fight or Flight reaction will be engaged when a verbal fight begins—it brings fear to those involved in the fight.

It gets more interesting (and complex). At the most basic level, a fight—physical or verbal—is a form of rejection. A member of the group is rejecting a core piece of the other individual. We are social beings and, therefore, exclusion from the group is a key fear of us as humans.

When we are rejected, we feel as though our being (physical or social) is threatened and in danger, and we need to survive. Here comes Fight or Flight to the rescue! Chances are that these type of discussion and pain will happen again in our lives. The next fight will be just as intense, if not more so, because the body mentally looks into the future to protect itself and can be stressed just expecting the pain will reoccur.

For example, it is like watching a scary movie... just with the simple idea of thinking about what might happen next in the scene, the tension builds up. Nothing has really happened yet, but our brain is preparing us. Our heart races, our palms become moist, our brain expects something to happen, and so it engages our Fight or Flight response before anything even appears on screen.

Just like in the movie, in your life you will have the same build-up happening when tensions are high or elevating. You've seen a scary movie before, therefore during the next scary movie your brain "looks" into the future and prepares to be scared, and your body prepares for anything and gives you a shot of adrenaline. It is true for scary movies, a tense discussion with a loved one, and at dinner parties. If you had an intense debate last month at a dinner party, this month as you sit at the table and someone mentions the upcoming election your brain will "look" into the future and see a Verbal Fight coming, and the body will prepare itself for action. This is valid in all our important relationships in our life—partners, friendships, work place relationships, home life, husbands, wives, and so on.

After the dinner party, in a calm and logical moment looking back, it seems silly to have thought/acted in that manner. That is exactly the point. Once that primitive part of the brain takes over and moves you away from rational thought, you move into Either/Or thinking, you **act** and stop thinking, not taking into account a wide variety of options to proceed. In a calm and safe place, you see many different forward options.

Also, in that calm moment, when you have passed the point when Fight or Flight was in control of the stressful situation, you can think of all the things you "should/could have said" or actions you "should not have done." Fight or Flight limits the use of critical thinking and logical brain, and constricts your thought in the short term.

This interaction is damaging to relationships with friends, co-workers and your most loved ones because the nature of Either/Or is so extreme. The most basic expression of Either/Or thinking is Fight or Flight... meaning a Verbal Fight (engaged) or a Verbal Flight (shut down) that can take over the relationship for years.

Over time these extreme points of view and actions can and will eat away the core and base of the relationship. So instead of growing closer together, the people engaged in the relationship will fight about the same thing over and over; the same fight, the same phrases and the same positions.

FIGHT OR FLIGHT! MAKE BETTER DECISIONS TO ENJOY YOUR LIFE QUICK WIN

Do Something Different and support (at the least acknowledge their position or right to a different point of view) each other's opinion.

The Either/Or mindset is a true fallacy. Life is filled with many options for every problem encountered. When the mindset is down to two options, then everyone loses. The individual, and couple, under these circumstances, is not a choice in life and basically is stuck with two losing options. At this point, there is no opportunity for growth and the ultimate goal of our relationships—dreams coming true—dies.

Here the bottom line is that each individual in a couple have different beliefs and mindsets about every topic. The fairytale life of the couple in complete agreement is false. Only when both individuals move out of Either/Or thinking, and into honoring that the other has their own valid opinion, will the relationship flourish.

Personally, I've been caught in an Either/Or mindset many times. Every time I chose to follow it through to the end, I lose. Only when I can sit back and see more options can I create a powerful growth experience.

> A simple example of an Either/Or mindset was a time my family decided we were to leave Florida and head back to Texas. We planned out the details with the trailer rental, packing, route, and all was set. I was sure that traveling for a few days in a car with our 2-year-old and our 1-year-old dog was a recipe for a lot of headaches and a painful drive…as if the long drive itself was not headache already.

> I decided I'd talk to my wife and I'd buy her and our two-year-old a plane ticket, and our dog and me would make the trip as quickly as possible so we could promptly meet in Texas. I just knew our 2-year-old would want to get out of his seat, and who could blame him? It can be very uncomfortable and unpleasant for long periods of time. My fears of uncertainty had taken over and were in full control.

> My wife said, no, we are going to make the trip as a family, with me and the dog, back to Texas. I froze, disagreed, and shut down. Fight or Flight was in control and my mind focused on Either/Or… Either I was going to get them on that plane, or I was going to have a miserable trip.

> I put the discussion aside for a few days, then brought it up again to my wife. I'd found tickets priced reasonably, and I was about to buy them for the move. She stayed in her position and explained that she was looking forward to the trip together, and it would be a good bonding and relationship builder. After all we were in this together.

> I'd not considered that it could be a relationship builder, not necessarily a miserable trip.
> In that moment I realized I'd built up the situation into a Fear of the Uncertainty and had put myself and my whole family into my Either/Or thinking. Neither of the Either/Or got me more of what I wanted: a closer relationship with my wife and child.

> I took a moment to step back and then I asked myself, what is the worst thing that could happen? If it didn't go well, we'd buy a plane

ticket for them at the nearest airport and I'd continue on the trip with our dog.

We made plans for the best-case scenario and drove fewer hours every day. We started very early while our son was still asleep. We took advantage of nap times. We stopped and had long play breaks. It was a complete success.

As I think about it, I got what I most wanted in this life, thanks to my wife for not falling into my Either/Or mindset. I could have missed a huge opportunity to have quality time and an experience with my family, due to an unfounded Fear.

While you should definitively use the powerful tool of Either/Or in dangerous situations, when it comes down to our closest relationships, make sure you move away from it, so it leads you to closer more full relationships and life.

---

1. BrightSight Speakers. (2014, August 19). *Matthew Lieberman: Social Pain is Real Pain*. YouTube. https://www.youtube.com/watch?v=pRgxqBw-0pE

FLIGHT

FLIGHT - EITHER/OR POSSIBLE EXAMPLES:

Either	Or
I emotionally close off	I fear I'll be hurt again
I shut down	I fear I'll not be heard
I give in again	I fear they will leave
I "let" them win	I fear my opinion doesn't count

In any of these examples above, the final action is to leave (mentally or physically). Many wrongly believe that the act of shutting down (leaving) is less damaging over years. While the Fight choice may seem harsher (and it might be in the moment), the Flight is deeply damaging for the individual and relationship over the longer term.

With the route of one partner choosing to stop emotional engagement, the other individual often thinks they've "won" the argument, but in truth this is very short-term thinking. Moving forward, the relationship has increasingly limited opportunity to grow because these two mindsets are habit forming and when the couple hits the next differing of opinion, then there is no place to go but back to emotional flight (shutting down) and/or fight. The habit will be followed and relied upon until one of the individuals brings it to consciousness and does something different.

Often one party will take steps to make the conversation environment "safer" which leads to shallow conversations that suck the life out of the love between two partners. It might look like this: they limit complimenting each other, have few or no discussions of ideas and growth, or they are just talking about the weather or a more dangerous conversation, the children. When the children become the only focal point between two individuals, they are left with no safe topics once the children leave home.

Is that type of interaction what you want for your life? What has happened to your wishes? Opinions? Dreams? Those are the topics of conversations we long to have with our mates.

The Either/Or mind set is a true fallacy for our conversations. Our relationships are filled with innumerable sets of opinions and potential challenging topics. When the mindset is focused on avoiding difficult conversations, to stay silent and shut down, everyone loses. At this point, there is no opportunity for growth, no vulnerability and the ultimate state of our relationships—a lifetime of dreams coming true—dies.

KEEPS RELATIONSHIPS IN FIGHTS

As shown already, the verbal disagreement from a loved one feels painful. This last sentence can seem extreme, but it is true. Especially with those few people in your lives with whom you work to be vulnerable and intimate.

How does Fight or Flight keep you stuck in (verbal) Fights in your closest relationships? Think about this simple example: One fine day you decide to share a closely held piece of your beliefs/ideas/opinions with a loved one. As you are sharing a key piece of who you are and what you value in life, you are constantly scanning the other individual's face and body language. If you perceive that your partner is (or even might be) in disagreement with what you are saying, and the possibility of verbal rejection of the information that you care about and trusted them enough to share, heightens. At this point you will likely feel emotionally fearful and in danger. Once the loved one makes a contradictory statement about your thoughts, the Fight is on!

Now if an emotional hit, regardless of the situation, happens once, then so be it, you will likely recover. However, when it happens over and over, recovery becomes more challenging and more ingrained. Logically, having the same fight over and over does not make sense. It's like hitting your head against a wall, expecting different results. The thing is that, yes, you have fights over and over, and, yes, you will have the same results no matter how hard you hit the wall. Everyone has been guilty of this action in relationships, That is one definition of insanity, when you do something over and over again and expect a different result.

At this point you might be wondering how you can move forward differently.

FIGHT OR FLIGHT! MAKE BETTER DECISIONS TO ENJOY YOUR LIFE QUICK WIN:

At a time of calmness in your life consider a different manner in which to communicate your opinion the next time conflict arises. For example, consciously choose not playing your part in having the same fight. You will be surprised. Calmness can bring clarity while in the middle of the fight, but clarity to act is challenging.

Please note that this is not about giving in to the other person; it is important to have your view too. It is worrisome and not good for a relationship when one member is always giving in. Those people are giving themselves away little by little, and one day there is nothing left to give and the relationship is done. The frightening part of this situation is that the relationship isn't "done" in a week or month, or even a year. Five or ten years later, when so much damage has been caused, then the problem is really tough to heal. To be fulfilled in a relationship, both parties must give and receive. It is a continuous cycle or circle.

Think again, What is the reason I'm in this relationship? Is it to continuously Fight for the next 10 years (or a whole life time) or to obtain resolution or a middle ground on a key issue? Is it to win at all costs?

Be very careful of moving to a place in your relationships of winning at all costs. Be aware when you move into this frame of mind, because you'll certainly cost yourself big. When you win, the other loses. Your loved one, the one you chose to spend your life with, loses… and frankly, both lose at that point.

Let's reverse the roles for a moment… do you like losing? Do you really want someone telling you what to do with your life every day? No and no. Do you really want a loved one to lose in life? No. You want to make up our own mind and live with the consequences. Yes! That is life and you want the same for your partner, for him/her to be living life to their fullest.

It's crucial to move out of a Win-Lose frame of mind and move into a place of acknowledgment. This is how relationships grow, with respect, and both parties start to obtain what is in their hearts. Trust and safety are fed to grow, and vulnerability is alive and well in that type of environment.

STAYING COMMITTED

In this section I address those in relationships who are committed to their vows, and at the same time engaged in continual Fight mode. I have suggested that you stop and change what has been keeping you stuck in fights as a couple.

The next logical question is how does one or both accomplish the change in state? How do you manage to change what you have created and possibly fed for so many years? Also, how do you influence someone else to move out of Fight or Flight state?

Step number one, and likely the most important, you must be assured that you are not engaged in a Fight or Flight frame of mind with this individual. Once you're committed to stay out of Fight or Flight, you'll take a lot of the unneeded energy out of the situation.

As you stay calm and level-headed, the other individual will change their actions/reactions. As the ground rules change (that is, the habit of fighting), the interaction will change and both will (slowly) gravitate toward a healthy place. The key reminder is that it takes two to fight.

Wrapped in this new mindset, it is important that you acknowledge the other's position on the issues. By acknowledging their opinion and position, you'll teach them how you want to be treated in the relationship. It takes time, but over weeks and months, the other individual will see a difference in the manner you engage. This typically leads to conversation about why you're not acting the same as in the past. When they see growth and change, then hopefully they will work to adapt to the new norm. Keep in mind you've been fighting this way for X number of months or years. It takes time to prove you've changed.

The next step is not about getting what you want in that moment with your mate in the instant of the conflict/discussion. It is about having more of what you desire in the relationship and life (Big Picture). Remember that Fight or Flight led people to make short term decisions (such as: prove your point, win the fight, make the other back down), and here you need to put it aside and focus on making long term decisions (such as: increasing trust, more love, move toward intimacy). As both individuals' ideas are honored, as both partners' thoughts are supported, as your beliefs grow, as both individuals' dreams come true, I guarantee the relationship will flourish. This is what we all want in our relationships. It takes time, is a slow at first, and then it will expand to become more.

Ultimately it is about removing the small arguments and disagreements from your relationship so the foundation is strengthened and you both grow closer. It is a choice; it is your choice. Do you want a relationship that focuses on small talk and unimportant topics? Do you want to move toward intimacy, building trust and dreams coming true? It starts with you and your decision to stay out of an adrenaline-fueled state.

KEEPS RELATIONSHIPS IN FLIGHT

The act of Flight, from an emotional perspective, can take many forms within a relationship. It can come across as almost harmless: emotionally shutting down, avoiding conflict, never standing ground on issues, always giving in to others or never asking for what they want. In all instances, the individual rarely shows their emotional side, and as time passes less and less of the individual seems emotionally alive. If this is you, be aware of (emotional) Flight, as it is one of the most damaging habits to set up in life.

I've known individuals who allowed emotional Flight to take hold in their life and openly admit they would change what they're saying and their opinions mid-sentence if they thought or perceived the other person was going to disagree with their point of view. Conflict, in any form, was not an option for them as they experienced disagreement as a rejection of who they were at their core.

It's understandable that running away from a fight might be seen as a best option in a specific circumstance. However, when running away and avoiding any type of conflict is **the only** option in your life or relationship, you'll end up running away your entire life. It will become a default or first choice.

Keep in mind that it may not be physically removing oneself or verbally stopping the interaction. It can also be an emotional choice. One can choose emotional Flight. They are (or you are) physically standing there, but emotionally distant and shut down.

In the short term, it is pretty easy to involve oneself in Flight. It is physically easy to leave a tense or heated argument/debate and mentally easy to emotionally switch off. In the short term, there are no problems. The argument is over (at least on the side of the person who runs) and there's been no damage to oneself or the relationship—again, with a very short-term viewpoint.

The absolute worst part comes with this as a long-term way of reacting. The inner-turmoil that is created can be a high cost to pay. The individual has given away their right to an opinion, has given away their desires, has given away their voice. All this for the benefit of feeling safe in the moment by running, by engaging in the Flight frame of mind. Over time it will emotionally drain the individual and steal their joy and life, not to mention its health consequences.

It has a huge cost and it will be paid not only by the persons who resort and allow themselves to adopt the emotionally passive choice of Flight. The relationship will also pay the price.

Let me tell you a story about this.

Two individuals came into my seminar a few months apart. An elderly gentleman was the first. Very early on he opened up and confessed that his wife of over 50 years of marriage had left him. His story was this: he was completely blindsided and had thought that all was fine in the relationship. He admitted he'd not checked in with her (ever) on how the relationship was working from her point of view. I encouraged him to work hard during the seminar for the next few days, and I was sure he'd find some of his answers.

From my point of view, it didn't take long to discover he was right; he was right about everything in his life.

A few months later I met an elderly woman in the same seminar room. I quickly realized she was the other half of the relationship. Her story was this: she'd spent over 50 years living in the place of always being wrong (his position of always right had set up hers as always wrong). Whenever she expressed her views, he'd shut her down and verbally prove to her why her ideas or desires would not work for them, and she took it as not only a rejection of her ideas and thoughts, but ultimately also as a rejection of her.

At some point of living more and more emotionally shut down, she could only think of two options (here it goes again, the mistaken quandary of Either/Or thinking): she could stay in the marriage shut down (emotional Flight) or she could cut all ties and leave him (another form of Flight). So she left, didn't take his calls, didn't contact him, didn't discuss it with anyone in her life.

Then she started to "live her life before she died." All the ideas, thoughts and dreams she'd expressed to him early in the marriage, which were all crushed, were now being accomplished. She did love her partner and wanted to return to the marriage but refused to return to what she experienced as an emotional void.
He'd made changes since returning from the seminar but she wanted to know if they would hold. Last I knew they were back together.

When one decides to fully engage in emotional Flight, where does that leave the other side of the relationship? Most likely fighting at all costs to "win." How fulfilling is it to be in relationship with someone who has no opinion, who has no voice? At the same time, how fulfilling is it to be in a relationship with someone who is bashing your opinion? This Fight or Flight will emotionally drain the individual, couple, and relationship.

The relationship pays a large cost in the most important areas. Consider common conflict topics, which could be avoided if one is constantly running away:

- Boundaries
- Children
- Money
- Sex

If these areas are to never find a common ground, a common place of understanding, where does that leave life and the relationship? In constant conflict or running away? Maybe one person makes all the decisions so the other is basically turned off?

Having your own thoughts, opinions, and dreams and believing in your own power to express them is a compelling manner in which to live life. All individuals deserve to live an open and compelling life. With your own point of view, it is not about pushing back and fighting it out "till death do us part." It is about finding the common point, in a safe and trusting environment. This is a starting point and the foundation of a dynamic relationship.

TRUTH ABOUT BOTH FIGHT AND FLIGHT

There is an unfortunate truth about relationships that engage in a Fight/Flight and Either/Or state. Habits or commonalities are formed such as, fighting about the same topic, fighting in the same manner, shutting down at the same point, and even the same hurtful lines. All of these factors lead to the relationship becoming stuck, and as time passes, growth and intimacy is choked off.

Think back to a current or former relationship in which Fight or Flight was an issue, and consider the reason you entered it. All close relationships start with the idea of becoming more, and enhancing both lives. Few of them stay in this frame of mind as Fight or Flight becomes more and more ingrained in the individuals.

Generally, after a fruitful start, relationships hit a wall and this occurs when one or both of the individuals share a closely held idea or opinion, and in this moment their mate doesn't conform to the wants and demands of the other. This is a key point in the relationship. When examined, looking into the past and removing any drama, from a healthy point of view, the relationship was possibly stuck in an unhealthy state. It might have been in this state for the past two, five or forty years. The key is to not allow it to become stuck and stay in place of purposeful choice and growth.

Let's look into what might happen to a marriage. I've seen that the most common bumps in relationships take place at three key moments.

1) First, approximately after two years of the relationship, if the couple has not set strong foundations beyond physical attraction, it can fall apart easily.

2) The next challenge is around year 7 or 8, approximately the time when the individuals understand they are not going to change their partner's habits and core beliefs. Often there is a false belief that the partner will, over time, begin to accept the "correct" way to live and think. By "correct," I mean your way. This is also perceived as a time when they will finally understand that the best way to live life is "just like me" meaning yours. This mindset causes increasing number of conflict points.

3) Finally, the most dangerous time is when the children leave home. The key topic of conversation over the previous 18 to 20+ years has been the

children. Then one morning you wake and there is a stranger across the table from you.

These three time points could be either scary or exciting.

All too often the relationship, at these key points, drifts into one or two places in the Fight or Flight spectrum. One individual gives themselves away to the other person or family (a form of emotional Flight). They don't speak up, but simply go along with everything or maybe simply believe that is the way it has to be in a life and relationship. It is a move into a life of coping. At some point, the other member of the relationship moves along with their life and gives up on going together and goes it alone. There may never be actual divorce, but the relationship is finished. The other side of the picture is never reaching common ground on big decisions or goals for the couple. No peace is to be had and the relationship moves into a Fight frame of mind on key topics.

These three key points can be filled with marvel about continuing to learn from one another and support each other in life. Learn to experience your partner as more than the physical (attractiveness); you must understand and respect their way of being, thoughts and beliefs. Lastly, find excitement in spending time and meeting your partner again, the person you married five, ten, or twenty years ago is not the same person today. The most important step is to continually build trust between you and your partner. This will greatly limit the number of Fight or Flight situations and help deter the length of the reaction. By choosing to be vulnerable with your loved one, and focusing on your life time dreams and moving toward them, as well as supporting the dreams of your loved one, you are living life! That is building a marvelous relationship, together!

While almost everyone agrees with the knowledge that all have differing opinions, we rarely live our lives that way. Consider the clear fact that no two people have the same thoughts and opinions. This is absolutely good news. Make the effort to honor their position and acknowledge that they have a right to experience the world in the manner they choose and see best.

REMEMBER THAT DISAGREEMENT DOES NOT EQUAL REJECTION. IN OTHER WORDS, IT IS NOT A FORM OF REJECTION THAT THE TWO OF YOU ARE NOT IN COMPLETE AGREEMENT. IT IS SIMPLY A DIFFERENCE IN HOW TO LIVE AND EXPERIENCE LIFE.

How do you react when your spouse disagrees with something that is important to you? Do you truly take their opinion into consideration for your decision? Or do you feel rejected and shut down (Flight) or move into conflict (Fight)?

The bottom line is that you're unable to change anyone's mind except your own.

The most frustrating activity in which couples engage is trying to change their partner's mind. It is a fruitless activity. Learn to appreciate where common ground occurs and acknowledge that there will be differences. Release the sense of feeling threatened by your loved one due to disagreement.

When you choose to see a differing opinion as anything more than that, there is a huge risk you'll move to a place of believing that disagreement is a rejection of you and/or the relationship. When this happens in the relationship, then one feels "attacked," and being attacked by the person you love the most is incredibly threatening. Then you move to the place of fear.

The goal for all healthy relationships, is that both individuals work to be emotionally and mentally healthy while supplying their full commitment. Combined with both individuals creating an environment of safety and trust, an incredibly fulfilling relationship is built. The last piece of the puzzle is vulnerability. Both individuals must know and understand the deep thoughts, ideas, dreams, goals of their loved one. In this state support of each other's life dreams, while reaching for their own, will create the relationship of your dreams. If this (or something similar) is not your goal, then take a look at the reason you're in the relationship in the first place.

FIGHT OR FLIGHT! MAKE BETTER DECISIONS TO ENJOY YOUR LIFE QUICK WIN

Understand, believe and live with the knowledge that disagreement does not equal rejection. Internally accept (and verbally express) that you acknowledge that your loved one has a right to their own thoughts, opinions and dreams.

I have my thoughts, opinions and dreams. My wife has her own thoughts, opinions and dreams. Also, we have our relationship dreams. I accept they don't all come into perfect alignment and choose to build safe and trust so we can support each other.

FLIGHT OR FIGHT BECOMES A (BAD) HABIT

Another key point of Fight or Flight is the risk of habit, and what happens in similar situations has similar reactions. We've touched on the risk of a Fight or Flight habit forming in the individual or relationship, and now we will look at it in detail. Our brains love habits; they allow us to repeat tasks or go through life with limited effort. Needless to say, we have good habits that move us forward and bad ones that keep us just where we are. The automatic choice to use a bad habit will remain until we consciously choose to remove it from our life and replace it with a good habit. Our loved ones have bad habits, as do we!

Be accountable for your bad habits and the damage you've caused. Now is the time to replace them with new loving habits.

Unfortunately, what your brain wants to do is use the habit (helpful or unhelpful) as much as possible, so that it doesn't have to work as hard. This leads to fixed behaviors and brings up a powerful point in this book: whenever you experience a similar situation **you react with a similar response** with little or no thought and energy required. For the purposes of this book, this means that if you've trained yourselves to have two options— a Fight or Flight response—then you've created a fixed behavior and habit that is not going to work well for you.

Here is a simple example. A sensitive topic is brought up and the immediate internal response is "Here we go again" and then one part of the couple says the lines of their "script" and the other person says their lines. It leads to the same fight, and never once did the person stop to see if the other was presenting new information. It is just a fight out of habit, and then it happens again and again. This type of habit setting is an easy trap to fall into in a relationship. Everyone who's been in this situation year after year knows this eats at the foundation of the relationship.

What is it worth to you to create a different outcome? To have a relationship that is safe and trusting? To have a new ending, you must have a new action at the beginning of the disagreement. Both individuals must be willing to create a trusting environment so that there is the opportunity for something different. Make a conscious choice right now about what needs to be changed.

FIGHT OR FLIGHT! MAKE BETTER DECISIONS TO ENJOY YOUR LIFE QUICK WIN

If you want a different you, a different outcome, you must consciously do something different and not fall into an old habit! How you do anything is how you do everything until you make a conscious decision to try something new.

Otherwise you're destined to the same ending, every time. When you're sick and tired of the same ending, and you want something different, then you have to be willing to do something different at the start. Don't allow your habits to run your life. Decide what you want the end point to be and create the actions "now" to arrive at that new desired space.

LACK OF HEALING FUNCTION

Be aware that within the Fight or Flight response, there is no innate desire to return and mend fences or check to make sure those involved are not emotionally/mentally hurt. There's a lack of a healing function of wounds created by the Fight or Flight response.

Logically, what is the purpose of repairing a relationship or friendship when (perceived) danger is present? None. However, when you've identified that it is not dangerous, but you've allowed fear to rule what happens to the encounter, once the adrenaline has exited your system, what happens next? Typically nothing; you "won" the encounter in one manner or another. The person standing on the top of the mountain (whether having fought their way or ran their way to the top) does not need to apologize to anyone!

There are certain topics in the relationship that are hot beds for potential conflict (finances, children, religion, politics, intimacy, etc.). However, they cannot be avoided as though they were trivial topics at a dinner party. They must be discussed and that leads to heated discussions, feelings of being right and no mechanism of going back and apologizing after the discussion. The topic (and conflict) is never finished and only likely to begin anew when addressed again.

After Fight or Flight has taken place, there is no innate desire to repair the pain caused in others. There is no ownership of issues and no accountability, only the goal of getting physically or emotionally safe. Thus, when individuals allow the Fight or Flight response to take place, and on top of that do not clean up the emotional mess they've caused, then safety and trust are eroded and the relationship dies a bit.

How often do you want to be on the losing end of a disagreement? How long would you stick around if there's no respect for your views? Adversely, how often do you want to see your significant other lose and die a little?

Sadly, if ever an instinct to return to make sure no one is emotionally dead or gravely (emotionally) injured, after a fight, too often, Round 2 becomes too easy to start. You don't want that person to be out of the fight forever, just lose that round.

In a moment of calm, every healthy person will admit that they want to have peace in their relationships, they want the best for the other individual and don't want to fight again. This is an important point. Data (and more and more research, the most famous being the 75+ year Harvard Study of Adult Development[1]) demonstrates that healthy social relationships are vital to a healthy longer life and stress reduction. These relationships can take the form of marriages, contact with friends and family, religious membership and group affiliations. Research shows that those with fewer social connections have a much higher death rate from illness. The final piece of information of this point is that social support for an individual meant there were fewer cardiovascular stress responses (Fight or Flight). You must purposefully heal your relationships damaged by Fight or Flight reactions.

Another fascinating example came from Robert M. Sapolsky author of *Why Zebras Don't Get Ulcers*, (pg 256) where he describes an example of "Stress-induced displacement of aggression." In the book the author gives an example of observing a male baboon losing a fight. After the lose, the baboon would then attack a weaker member of the group to release his aggression.

As humans, we act in similar destructive functions: we are frustrated, pick fights, are emotionally cold to those around us because another area of our lives isn't working well. These actions will not bring healing to any relationships. However, in the moment, we are (emotionally) hurting and may choose to hurt others.

How do you arrive home after a challenging long day, or long week at work? Do you meet the family with the love you have for them, or do you walk in distant and possibly short on patience?

In dangerous situations, there is no need for healing the relationship or situation. Contrarily, in emotionally fearful situations (not endangering), healing of the actions and words are vital to the long-term health of the relationship. You can choose to use new tools and limit the impact of Fight or Flight in your relationships (and interactions), or you can learn tools to heal the damage caused post-engagement. Moving to a "win" frame of mind only creates a "lose" for the loved one. Learn a healthy manner to apologize for your part of the damage. Learn communication skills to communicate more clearly and openly. Heal past hurts so that they don't appear in today.

---

1. Mineo, Liz. (2017, April 11). The Harvard Gazette. "Good genes are nice, but joy is better."   News.harvard.edu/gazette/story/2017/04/over-nearly-80-years-harvard-study-has-been-showing-how-to-live-a-healthy-and-happy-live/

PART 4: THE END OF FIGHT OR FLIGHT

There is no way to completely end Fight or Flight in your life (nor would you want to in all situations). It is a part of you as much as breathing and an import part of keeping you safe and alive. You can control what you do with your decision-making process once you realize you're in a Fight or Flight situation. You can take steps to keep it from ruining life's experiences and relationships. Make a different decision that is more fruitful instead of continuing on the same path. For some situations, you can prepare yourself mentally beforehand and recognize that you're not in a dangerous setting. When adrenal glands start to work, try to regain control. Finally, once the situation has passed and you can acknowledge that your decision came from a Fight or Flight frame of mind, then you can remake the decision if needed.

Take time and search for your answer to determine if you will be, or are now, in a dangerous situation. When you can internally resolve that you're in a Fearful situation, then these questions and decision points that follow will set you up for closer relations, healthier actions, and the ability to build safety and trust.

Returning to the boxer analogy presented earlier, the points that follow will allow you to become trained at handling foreseen and unforeseen fearful events in your life. You'll leave the days behind when you simply reacted to the individual or situation. With practice, clarity will present itself, and perhaps those difficult situations will diminish in power. The long-term goal is to build a healthier relationship and become closer to those key people in your life.

It is absolutely within your control to stop Fight or Flight from ruining your life. By now you've seen that it causes great harm mentally and physically. Plus, it eats away at the trust and safety needed in long-term relationships. It robs you of life's smallest sweetest moments and of potential wins. All due to perceived fear which our bodies and brains believe is danger.

The end of allowing Fight or Flight to ruin your life starts right here with your awareness of the challenging relationships in your life. When making the choice to blame others for the situation, there is no personal accountability. You're basically saying "I'm helpless to their acts, actions and my reaction/s." This mindset is not true; there is always another option and choice you can make. Your actions are within your control and you decide if you're going to allow fear to run your life or to make a choice to live the cleanest life possible and act to your highest standards.

End Fight or Flight; it doesn't belong in your daily life. To end Fight or Flight ruining your life, you must engage the reasoning part of your brain as quickly as possible. I strongly suggest you go through these next chapters when you are in a calm place and can think about what is important in and for your life. If you attempt to put this into action when you are in the heat of a battle, it is difficult.

Use the following steps to introduce a healthier way of interacting in your daily relationships. The following questions and main points will create a safe trusting place within yourself and your loved one.

- Breathe
- Establish Safety and Trust
- What type of life do you want for yourself?
- What type of life do you want for your loved ones?
- What type of relationship do you want to live in?
- What do you want to teach others and your children about relationships?
- How will you act in your next Fight or Flight situation?
- What do you truly fear?

We'll go deeper into each point in the following chapters.

BREATHE

Breathe. Please breathe slowly.

Remember this one thing to get your mind and body under control along with your Fight or Flight mechanism—take a big breath.

Start with breathing, because it is your main tool. It helps you get ready for a future encounter where you'd normally move into Fight or Flight, and it helps you regain center in the midst of a fearful situation.

Over years of study and experience, I've seen a few options to get the mind out of Fight or Flight in a quick and healthy manner.

Breath is part of life and feeling alive, but few are trained to see the benefits of breathing deeply and consciously. At key points in your life, conscious breathing will bring the benefit of calmness to you and the situation. This is due to the fact that the pay-off for a big deep breath is the first huge step to re-engage the logical brain.

Some of the other manners that society uses to get the nervousness presented by Fight or Flight under control are: substances (both legal and illegal; both doctor-prescribed and the street variety). It also happens in stress-related illnesses and avoidance (avoid situation and avoid life). All of these are simply bad patterns used to avoid pain/stress/fear and keep Fight or Flight from firing. All are incredibly damaging to our bodies and lives, plus they are only temporary fixes that do nothing to manage the situations or the discomfort. Conversely, by avoiding issues, the bad habits grow and become more powerful while humans using them weaken. Thus, important and necessary, is to return to conscious breathing as your best ally. It is beneficial in many ways and there are numerous powerful breathing techniques—Abdominal Breathing, Breath Prayer, Cleansing Breathing, to name only a few.

I find, personally, if I take one deep breath, it will quickly refocus my thoughts. More accurately, it allows me to think logically instead of keeping an Either/Or frame of mind.

Numerous doctors and experts have written about techniques that work best for them. Dr. Esther Sternberg (physician & author) used an in-the-moment technique to train the body's reaction to stressful situations and dampen the production of harmful stress hormones. She says rapid breathing is controlled by the sympathetic nervous system. It's part of the "Fight or Flight" response—the part activated by stress. Therefore, in the act of slowing your breath, you counteract the Fight or Flight response.

Rapid breathing is an excellent self-awareness sign that you're in a Fight or Flight fearful situation. Train yourself to pay attention to a change in breathing pace. It will give you a cue that the primitive part of your brain has taken over and encountered fear or danger.

For some, meditation, or a similar means, can be an incredibly effective and powerful tool to prepare for Fight or Flight moments in the future. Herbert Benson, in *The Relaxation Response*, used scientific research to show that short periods of meditation, using breathing as a focus, could alter the body's stress response. There are numerous options; find what works best for you.

Have you ever caught yourself holding your breath in the middle of situations? Besides rapid breathing, this is another cue telling you that you are Fight or Flight mode.

For me, the second I'm forced to take a deep breath out of a need to survive is the time I acknowledge that I'm in a situation where I need to take a second and think. Before I even ponder "What is my next step?" I take in a huge breath.

What breath does from the very onset is to start the relaxation process. It slows the heart rate, lowers blood pressure, allows the brain to engage, and disengages emotional drive. While it does feel relaxing, it is more about bringing internal balance to the situation and removing you from two options to as many options as you chose to entertain.

Robert M. Sapolsky states in *Why Zebras Don't Get Ulcers* (pg 414); "I would apply the 80/20 rule to stress management—80 percent of the stress reduction is accomplished with the first 20 percent of effort. The mere act of making an effort can do wonders."

I love this insight, and if we apply it here, the simple act of forcing yourself to take a few deep breaths will increase the chances of moving yourself out of Fight or Flight and into an action that will build and strengthen your relationships. It will allow you to improve every area of your life from making the best decision for your career to demonstrating to the children in your life how healthier actions look. It is a powerful and easy step to obtain an 80 percent remedy to the situation.

FIGHT OR FLIGHT! MAKE BETTER DECISIONS TO ENJOY YOUR LIFE QUICK WIN

Next time you face a physical, emotional or mental situation where you can feel your pulse race, your muscles tense, take a Deep Breath! Only positive can come out of the action. It will allow the logical part of your brain to engage and then you can make the best decision for you in the moment.

In graduate school, I faced the biggest project in my life. It lasted all semester long, and for the final project, each group had to sit in a large auditorium and answer questions from a panel of (professionals) judges. It was stressful, and believe me, may times I wanted to engage the flight mechanism and run for the beach. My parents came into town to support me for the panel. My mother passed me a note right before I took my seat.

It simply said: Breathe.

And it worked.

I took breath after breath. I could feel my pulse lower, I could feel my voice increase and my tone strengthen.

My Fight or Flight response did not serve me well in my graduate courses. It would not have served me that night. Only by taking back control of my body and engaging my logical brain did I prove myself, step through my fear and deliver the true me.

While writing this book, and based on my life experience, my wife and I decided to pass along the gift of breathing to our son. When he's facing a stressful or painful situation, we first encourage him to take a deep breath. He'll forever have the gift of taking a deep breath when he feels his Fight or Flight response kicking in. I hope that it will become automatic, and in the near future, he won't even realize it is happening.

I remember one clear example of us sitting at breakfast with my wife's aunt. It was the three of us and our son. We were enjoying the morning, and our son was just three years old. Another boy (a bit older) was also in the restaurant and our son invited him to play at our table. Our son had brought a few of his favorite toys.

He had a brand-new truck with him, and he was focused on putting it through three-year-old stress tests (that is, normal play). My wife slipped away from the table for few minutes. Her aunt and I continued the conversation. As our food arrived, we all became distracted and the next thing I know I'm staring into the eyes of my son and they are communicating almost terror. I quickly realize, as my son's eyes start to fill with tears, that the other boy had the new truck.

Perfect teaching for conscious breathing example. I quietly instructed him to take a deep breath with me. We breathed in and out a couple times. Then I asked him what was wrong and how he'd like to remedy the situation. He politely asked for the toy back from the other boy and life went on happily.

My wife's aunt observed the entire exchange and commented on how impressed she was and how well our son handled the situation. "I thought he was going to break down right there at the table and get his toy back."

That is the exact point of how it is to allow Fight or Flight to take over your life. Did our son have the beginnings of Fight or Flight arouse inside of him in this encounter? Absolutely, but by calming himself and engaging his thinking brain, he could make the very best choice for him.

The most important benefit of training yourself to breathe is the vantage point of multiple options. As you've seen with Fight for Flight, when it kicks off inside of you, your vision and mindset narrow down to two options. When you give yourself the option to breathe, you give yourself the opportunity to see beyond two options and instead hold multiple options. Getting past the two-option viewpoint is the tricky part. Once you've trained yourself to see more, you'll see a lot more!

Breathing is incredibly impactful not only for yourself, but also for those in your life. If you encounter a friend or loved one who's in a Fight or Flight situation, instruct them to breathe. My favorite phrase is to give a command, "Breathe deeply with me. Breathe in" (and I take an exaggerated breath). Then I tell them to hold it hold it and release. I repeat the process a few times.

The most important benefit of training yourself to breathe is the vantage point of multiple options. As you've seen with Fight for Flight, when it kicks off inside of you, your vision and mindset narrow down to two options. When you give yourself the option to breathe, you give yourself the opportunity to see beyond two options and instead hold multiple options.

Getting past the two-option viewpoint is the tricky part. Once you've trained yourself to see more, you'll see a lot more!

Breathing is incredibly impactful not only for yourself, but also for those in your life. If you encounter a friend or loved one who's in a Fight or Flight situation, instruct them to breathe. My favorite phrase is to give a command, "Breathe deeply with me. Breathe in" (and I take an exaggerated breath). Then I tell them to hold it hold it and release. I repeat the process a few times.

The most important benefit of training yourself to breathe is the vantage point of multiple options. As you've seen with Fight for Flight, when it kicks off inside of you, your vision and mindset narrow down to two options. When you give yourself the option to breathe, you give yourself the opportunity to see beyond two options and instead hold multiple options. Getting past the two-option viewpoint is the tricky part. Once you've trained yourself to see more, you'll see a lot more!

Breathing is incredibly impactful not only for yourself, but also for those in your life. If you encounter a friend or loved one who's in a Fight or Flight situation, instruct them to breathe. My favorite phrase is to give a command, "Breathe deeply with me. Breathe in" (and I take an exaggerated breath). Then I tell them to hold it hold it and release. I repeat the process a few times.

ESTABLISH TRUST AND SAFETY

What is the opposite of the feeling of Danger and Fear? The feeling of **Trust and Safety**.

Do you feel trust and safety in your relationships? Without an environment of trust and safety in the relationship, workplace, household, and internally in the individual, the opportunity to build a stronger deeper relationship is stunted. There is limited space for healthy change to be created. In order to get the most out of your relationships, you must build and rebuild a trusting and safe environment. Because without trust and safety, you can move very quickly into a Fight or Flight reaction, and a Fearful situation could lead you into the feeling of a Dangerous situation very easily.

Fear vs. Danger, Danger vs. Fear. Thus far we've established that distinguishing between the two is of utmost importance to understand whether Fight or Flight is an appropriate reaction to the situation. Let's examine some different areas and see how Trust and Safety, versus lack of it, might impact the situation:

IN YOUR RELATIONSHIP

Disagreement, fights, misunderstandings are all normal parts of a long-term relationship. However, when an environment of daily disagreement in the relationship is established as a habit and becomes a frequent event, then the base of the relationship erodes.

Additionally, we've looked at how disagreement can be experienced as a "hit." It is an emotional hit, but it can still be experienced in a somewhat dramatic feeling.

No two individuals have the same experience, thoughts, or opinions about a single topic, but, you must come to a place of healthy conflict. You must trust that the other individual will stay by your side "tomorrow" in the midst of the disagreement and you must give your partner that same trust.

If that basic place of trust does not exist, then fear and doubt sets in. With fear and doubt, there is a higher likelihood that you will go into a Fight or Flight defense. This leads you right back to an either/or frame of mind. The conflict begins and you have a fight about the same topic, pretty much in the same order, saying the same things to one another. Or one of the individuals emotionally and verbally shuts down (Flight) and the relationship dies slowly. Sounds familiar? Hope not for too long.

With trust and safety, a couple can work through the disagreement and acknowledge the other's position. Without it, Fight or Flight is too powerful a reaction and it continues to ruin your relationship.

Are you truly in danger with your loved ones? Choose to act accordingly in your next encounter.

IN YOUR PROFESSION

What type of work environment is created when there is no trust in the office or organization? Does the leadership foster a place where new ideas are accepted with open arms, and not squashed? Without trust that the right thing will happen, or safety for each individual, the organization comes to a state where it is only as good as one person at the top. The organization suffers and will not reach its full potential.

Are you truly in danger in your profession? Choose to act accordingly in your next encounter.

IN YOUR FRIENDSHIPS

Without trust and safety, the friendship will not grow. Do you offer a safe place for your friends to share with you? Do you feel scared to death to share who you truly are and what you truly think? If there is no room for trust and safety, you'll be left talking about nothing of importance (also known as chit chat) because there is a risk that someone will be (emotionally) hurt with no repair. What type of friendships do you want in your life? Are they life-long deeply profound connections in which you grow, or just acquaintances?

Are you truly in danger with your friends? Choose to act accordingly in your next encounter.

In all of the previous examples, without trust and safety, Fight and Flight are much more likely to happen and exist more frequently. While we cannot be responsible for others' actions in the relationship, we can ensure that our words and actions fully build the environment in which we want to live and experience life.

If you live in a relationship without trust and/or safety, then change your position and create it. Not once, not twice, but forever more. When you change your actions, others are forced to change their actions. The payoff is potentially huge. It will move you from a place of being stuck to a place of growth and allow both parties to get more of what they want out of the relationship. Think about this so you can be mentally ready for upcoming encounters.

WHAT TYPE OF LIFE DO YOU WANT?

Once you've taken that huge cleansing breath and you've started the process of regaining control of your Fight or Flight response, consider the following questions and then **act** in a manner that creates safety and trust between the parties involved.

The first question is: "**What type of life do I want?**"

Big picture: In its most simple form, you have a choice every moment of every day. "Do I want to live more or die little by little?"

You don't have the choice to stay right where you are. You either grow or die in every moment on this earth. The good and interesting news is that when you feel your Fight or Flight response arouse, then that is the most basic proof you are alive and living life to the fullest in the moment!

And as human beings, you have the privilege of using your logical brain and asking questions such as: What type of life do you want? This allows you the opportunity to live life, grow and fully engage.

I understand that, at times, it is hard to know exactly what you want… and often it is easier to know what you do not want. With that said, let me ask you a counter-question: Do you want more Fight and Flight in your life? The feelings and actions associated with that circumstance of life are: fewer loving relationships, talking about things of minimal importance, fewer dreams coming true, feeling less than you might otherwise, and so on. I trust your answer is an absolute NO! in your heart and brain. You want more, bigger dreams, and closer relationships.

However, to get there you need growth and change, and that is often uncomfortable, when life pushes you to the point of newness, often Fight or

Flight kicks in. Thus if you can breathe through it and then regain control, you can decide to choose growth and change and embrace the newness.

"What type of life do you want?" is one of the most simple, aggravating, important and difficult decisions you'll ever make in your life:

1) To have clarity on what you want in your life and relationships and

2) What you'll have to do different in order to obtain it

It's a simplistic question with a lifetime of ramifications. Just as vital is the fact that not asking the question or answering it will lead to a loss of focus on where you really desire to go and how you want to live.

Without clarity on what you want, it is increasingly unlikely that it will be obtained. You must focus your mind on what type of relationship and what aspects of a relationship are important to you. Decide what is important and aim to have those aspects fulfilled in your life.

There are a few places to start your search for your answers. Do you want more:

- Trust - what will your actions have to be in order to be more trusted and trustworthy?

- Love - how does a woman or man who is loving speak to loved ones and family?

- Peace - when a truly peaceful person is faced with a fearful situation, how would they react?

- Respect - what actions will have to take place to give respect in your life?

Remember, what you give is what you receive. Therefore, if you want trust, love, peace, and respect, you have to first give that trust, love, peace, respect.

Are you open to giving these to others in your life? Just because I want more peace in my life doesn't mean it will happen. I cannot expect others to bring it to me, if I cannot create it within myself. I have to be responsible for creating it in every aspect possible in my life. Then others have the possibility to add to that experience.

We must know what type of relationship we want to have and live in our daily life. This is key because, in so many ways, our relationships are our life. We must practice how we want our relationships to become reality with everyone in our life. There is no picking and choosing of how to act and be with people in general.

The human brain is fascinating; it is really powerful at moving toward something. With focus it can help you to obtain the goals in your life. It is horrible at moving away from something. If you don't want something, it is poor at hitting the target. It needs a forward point to move toward.

If you're fearful of something in your life, such as true love, true attachment, that peace doesn't exist. Then you'll find it increasingly difficult to obtain. The brain needs a target. With the fearful belief that an experience doesn't exist, you'll only see what doesn't exist and never what does.

This is a high-level question for life, and it starts with your actions and decisions right now and every day forward. Once you have clarity on your situation, you can focus on how to instill it on a daily and moment by moment level. Only one person can create the life they want. And that person is you.

WHAT TYPE OF LIFE DO YOU WANT
FOR YOUR LOVED ONES?

At times, in life, it is easier to put your loved ones first. If the previous question was a challenge to answer, now I ask you: What type of life do you want for your deeply loved ones? Do you want them living in a constant Fight or Flight mode? Do you want their life-long dreams to come true, so they too can live in passion and joy?

Let me start with this story.

> I've learned that when things go bump in the night, or I return from a long trip, the best action I can take is to check every inch of the house (or seek out the "bump"). This allows me to put that fear to rest and calm my Fight or Flight instinct. It is also a lesson my wife and I have passed onto our son.

> When he was four, there was a specific evening in the late fall when the family headed upstairs and he stayed downstairs for a few minutes. I heard his coming upstairs quickly (not strange for a four-year-old) and he entered the bedroom. The look on his face told me that something was not right! I asked him and he stared at me a then said, "I hear a sound of something moving behind me downstairs."

> I've worked with him about facing fears so they don't grow, and using the technique of seeking out what caused the fear, I said, "Let's go downstairs and see what we can find that made the noise so you're not scared any longer. I started to walk toward the stairs, but he didn't move. I walked back and said, "Come on, buddy."

> He said, "No."

I said, "I'll go alone and check it out."

That is exactly what I want for my loved ones. I want them to face their fears and put them to rest, so they don't become bigger and bigger.

While an individual's experience in this world is out of our control, we can control our actions with that person. If we choose to create love for our mate, children, or close friends, we can do whatever is in our power for them to have love when we are close.

Their experience with the world is one thing; another is their experience with us.

When tensions arise with your loved ones, what do you want them to feel or experience in that moment? Will you face tension again? Yes! Does it have to be the same ending every time (Fight or Flight)? No! You can choose to act in a different manner so that they feel loved, at peace, respected, with worth no matter what the emotional stress is at the moment.

In my personal experience, as my dreams came true, I became a better husband. As my wife supported me in my dreams, I was overly committed to supporting her in her dreams. I want a wife who's excited about life. Who's dreaming for more, and who is filled with passion, not with fears and Fight or Flight responses.

With this truth, I decided I must do my part to create that environment with and for her. What I do want for my wife is more love. When we have conflict, it is up to me to take a deep breath and move out of Fight or Flight and into a frame of mind to find resolution. I consciously cannot run to dangerous thoughts "She'll leave me", "she will beat me" or "she's controlling me." We have both worked to make this relationship a safe place for us. With that breath, I know I'm safe with her and I know I can trust her to hear me. No need to yell or shut down. For me, personally, the only thing more damaging than allowing myself to move into Fight or Flight is to have both of us in that frame of mind. Then nothing is accomplished.

I don't want a relationship where we default to talking about the weather and children. I want a relationship where we share our ideas, opinions and dreams. I want my loved ones to have their dreams come true and I'll play a part in making it happen.

So I ask you again, what type of life do you want for your deeply loved ones?

My four-year-old son wants to be a super-hero and he chooses to be all super-heroes combined (led by Spider-man, but it changes now and then). What are the chances of this happening? Probably zero to none. However, I can and choose to support him in his dream. I want him to continue to dream in life. Yes, it would be easy to pat him on the head, ignore his dream, or crush it. But I want him to move forward in that dream. I have no idea where it will end for him, but I do know dreaming in life has incredible value.

Therefore, I play "super-heroes" with him and I allow him to be and do whatever he wants in the moment. We talk about Spider-man and I allow him to ask questions about him, and when I don't know the answer, we look it up. He'll never be Spider-man per se, but his boyhood dream could lead him to into pursuing his dreams once he's older.

With this, all I am trying to say is that, in life, you could have every opportunity to support your loved ones on their path to dreams coming true and you could also have every opportunity to kill those dreams. What do you choose to do?

Now bring your thoughts back to yourself. Think back to the early stages of any dear/close relationship. I'm sure you had big beautiful dreams for yourself, for the relationship and for your partner. Are you keeping the space alive for those dreams to come true? Have you held that original mindset for true intimacy and passion for life?

What do you want for your loved one? When you answer that question, your actions will fall into line.

WHAT TYPE OF RELATIONSHIP DO
YOU WANT TO LIVE IN?

There are three entities in our personal relationships. They are: yourself, your partner (friendship, children, work place, parents) and the relationship. We must take care of all three. It is up to each member of the committed relationship to give their 100 percent in the relationship to create what is important to them. Note that it is not a 50 percent and 50 percent; it is 100 percent and 100 percent. And this holds true in the good and the bad times.

Give your 100 percent in the co-creation of a beautiful, thriving relationship. Start by giving, if you want a respectful relationship, then when times are loving, show respect for others. More important, when there is stress on the relationship, show a lot of respect for the other individual.

Also remember that just because there is disagreement on a topic, it does not mean that there has to be disrespect. Each person can and should have their own opinion on each situation. To believe you'll both have the same opinion, or worse, to believe that if you disagree, then there is no love, will only lead to feeling unloved in the relationship. For sure there will be disagreement. Welcome disagreement with a manner of respect, love and openness and your relationship will foster more of what you want.

WHAT TYPE OF RELATIONSHIP DO YOU WANT TO
LIVE IN?

It is up to you to create and give to the relationship what you want.

Now that you know what type of relationship you want to live in, you must be clear on what your ground rules are. It is too easy to fall into the trap of Fight or Flight in the heat of the moment or in the middle of an argument. But making a decision and a plan right now about how you'll react, while calm, will head off the urge to run to a more destructive action. That will help you get to a good place as a person and as a couple.

Note that such rush of adrenaline can be as hooking to an individual as a drug. To feel the rush of energy and focus can lead to looking for more of it. It can also become a habit in the relationship. Then one day, a few years down the road, nothing has been accomplished in the relationship except hurt and destruction. And both will be stuck in the rerun of the fight over and over again—saying the same things, shutting down, not listening, and simply looking for the counter point and drifting further apart from your mate.

Always keep in mind that if you want a different outcome to a situation, you must do something different in the moment. Which outcome will give you more of what you want in your life and relationship? Fighting again to make sure you are right, or acknowledging their point of view and choose to come together to find a solution? How do you make those dreams come true, including the dreams of the relationship?

What type of relationship do you want to live in?

Start now.

WHAT DO YOU WANT TO TEACH
YOUR CHILDREN?

The fourth question for most of us to answer (considering your children, nieces, nephews and/or grandchildren) is: **What do you want to teach your children?**

This is a huge game changer for me. First, it does not matter if you have children today, if your children are grown, or if you've chosen to never have children of your own. On some level, there are children in your life and they are watching.

Upon arrival into this world, or your home, you're creating or impacting their habits which will create their home in years to come. Start to teach and lead with purpose and focus, and do it now. Don't wait, because once the habits are ingrained, they are not easily changed. The first place to start is your Fight or Flight response, children don't need to unnecessarily experience the automated response from their parents/loved ones.

My son is watching everything and learning for his life everything I do with my life. For me to instill the belief that I'm in danger, or we are in danger, doesn't serve him in his life, unless we really are. I believe that when faced with true danger, his instincts will kick in fiercely and he'll do well. However, on a daily basis, allowing fear or danger to drive thoughts and control decisions does not lead him to the healthiest life possible. I choose to create a strong foundation that unsure situations are to be faced head on and calmly. This skill will serve him in a positive manner his entire life, not to mention the huge benefits it will bring to me and my health.

On the other side, if your child is grown, they are still watching you. They are still learning from you no matter what age they are. They will be your age some day and you are teaching them how to live their lives when they are your age. If you use Fight or Flight to battle with your partner, or your parent, then they will likely act in the same manner with the partner and you, the parent.

Here's something simple I noticed as I watch my parents and grandparents age. I often wonder if I'll ever retire. I've pondered this to a great extent over the past years. A great-grandmother of mine owned rental properties until she was 80, only to sell them once she remarried! One set of my grandparents were farmers and worked every day well into their 70s. Another grandmother was fully engaged in their business and traveling internationally in her early 80s. My parents seem to be on a similar path.

I'm watching and learning the pros and cons of never retiring. If I don't make a conscious decision, most likely I'll automatically do the same thing they've done with their lives and work. I'm still learning from them with every life decision.

When I think about the type of family I want my children to live in, I want it to be as safe and stable as possible. This leads me to act healthier with my loved ones, and make the best decision possible for my body. I had no idea how much life could change for the better with children.

Additionally, if they see parents fight, they will believe that is what happens in relationship and will create the same in their life. They will create what they know.

You will create what you know, unless you put forth the effort to do something different, and live in reason and choice instead of Fight or Flight.

Now don't forget there is a larger viewpoint that is at stake with your children. Growing up in a constant state of Fight or Flight home life will have a negative life-long impact on their relationships and health. Choose not to live in a home full of fear and Fight or Flight. According to Dr. Robert Sapolsky in *Why Zebras Don't Get Ulcers*: (pg 348), "Thus acute stress increases the reinforcing potential of a drug." In the book, he outlines an experiment in which a pregnant rat is put into stressful situation. In such environment her offspring will more than likely opt for drug use as an adult. While not a perfect parallel, there is no doubt that unhealthy stresses in the home life will lead to unhealthy impacts in adulthood.

Right now, you're setting up life-time habits for the children in your space. The more you demonstrate fear in the home, and the more you rely on your Fight or Flight mechanism, the more chances they'll have serious challenges late in life. Today you're setting them up for life.

HOW WILL YOU ACT IN YOUR NEXT CONVERSATION (AND LIFE)?

The fifth question to answer for yourself, that will mentally prepare you to have a different encounter is: How should I act in my next conversation and life? Right now, in complete calmness and away from sweaty palms, racing heart, and quickening breath, is the time to decide; it will play a huge role in your key relationships.

Some other questions that could be helpful for you as you work on finding your answers are:

What type of person do you want to be in life, in your key relationships?

What do you want your world to look like, and how do you want to be treated?

It is up to you to make this happen and it starts with your next conversation.

Next time the situation arises, and the tension goes up, and the adrenaline starts to flow, how will you act and react? What do you want that next conflict-filled interaction to look and feel like? Take a moment, close your eyes and make the decision right now on how you'll carry yourself in the world and live it out.

Something important to consider is while it is true that the vast majority of people don't want to seem weak, meaning they don't want to be the ones constantly "giving in," the bottom line on that point is: avoid/ STOP making big deals about little deals. In other words, if it is of no consequence to you in a moment of calm, then don't blow up and allow Fight or Flight to ruin your life in the moment of the disagreement.

At the moment of encounter, when the disagreement (about something small or nothing) starts, then:

Step 1: **BREATHE**

Step 2: Use a phrase that is non-combative to **de-escalate** the argument. Such as: I understand your point, I acknowledge your position, I hear what you're saying.

Step 3: **Acknowledge** you've strengthened the relationship and moved out of Fight or Flight and into having more choices, peace and stability.

You want to do this to save your relationship, because it is possible to fight your relationship away. You can drive such a wedge into it that the flame that keeps it going will die. The relationship can go on a long time. It can even go on forever, however, the original passion, love and drive of the relationship will be gone. This is also true for any important bond in your life, siblings and friends.

Please note, if it is important issue for you and your relationship, by all means go ahead and have healthy conflict. It is not necessary that you always agree. However, it is absolutely necessary that you remove Fight or Flight from the discussions, and that you breathe and work to find a common understanding.

What happens if despite all mentioned above, and despite you having to do your mental preparation, things don't go as planned, and adrenaline wins one round and you fall into Fight or Flight? Don't stay down. Get up and continue to create the life you want, and focus on what you want in your next conversation.

Change will not happen immediately, and it will not be immediately reciprocated either. It takes time, but it all starts now. Think about it. If you've been living in Fight or Flight for the last 10 years, one fight, where old habits are not in control, will not cause a visible earthquake of change. However, when you change how you handle conflict in the relationship, the earthquake of change will be taking place within you. Only then, little by little, the way conflict is handled in the relationship will change.

Right now is the time to make the decision on how you'll handle the next piece of conflict. You know it is coming, you've had the same fight before and will have the same fight again. You've been there before and in a matter of time you'll be there again. I encourage you to choose strength, do not go the weak route in which one looks for excuses and others to blame. All is under your control as long as it is within your skin.

WHAT DO YOU TRULY FEAR?

The sixth and last question to ask yourself is: **What do I truly fear?**

It is the question behind the question that truly gives us more insight into our reactions. When you are experiencing Fight or Flight, what are you fearing?

Some examples follow:

- That you might come across as weak? Can this be linked to your early life or previous relationship?

- That she/he will leave you if you defy? Is that a realistic possibility or based on past experience? Have you had this discussion and asked directly?

Once you gain awareness regarding your biggest fear in life, then you bring clarity to many of your interactions and the manner in which you handle them. Finding what you fear will allow you to deal with it, work on it, and speak your truth, whereas if you choose to hide it, and allow it to grow inside of you, at some point it will come out as anger.

The next profound question is: Where in my life do I allow my fear to exist? Even if you think you are pushing it down, it does not go away.

To some extent, I personally allow it to exist in my finances. I allow it to impact my financial decisions. I allow it to keep me stuck from making decisions. It drives me to save and be prepared for "what if." It drives me to over save and prepare for too many "what ifs." Therefore, I see the worst-case scenario when an unexpected financial event occurs, which leads to my fears increasing and fights with my loved ones (unexpected credit card charges, big budget house expenses, or our budget).

Another of my deepest held fears that I allowed to run my life for too long was: "I never want to make a mistake." I truly believed it would never get fixed. Even today, I can still feel the fear creep up on me if something unexpected appears in my life. Instead of allowing my Fight or Flight mechanism to kick in, I choose to consciously breathe and ask myself the question behind the question. Put the fear aside and use my logic to find the best solution out of many.

By identifying my truest fears, I can observe that my life works better. I know the fears are there; we all have them. Understand what they are and see how they push you to make poor decisions, so at the very least, you are able to influence them. Put you fears to rest when you know a better option is available for you.

WHAT DO YOU REALLY FEAR?

The above six questions are meant to help you think about Fight of Flight while calm, thus helping you to consciously decide how you will react and handle the interaction in the midst of the unexpected event, which if left unchecked will start the adrenaline flowing.

In other words, once you decide what your fears are really about and what you really want from life in a calm moment, then you will be ready to handle the situation differently the moment Fight or Flight starts creeping in on you. You will move away from having the same Fight, or moving to a place of Flight, and into health and more in your daily interactions and relationships. These questions and key points will create a safe trusting place within yourself and your loved ones.

The end of allowing Fight or Flight to ruin your life starts right here with the awareness of the challenging relationships in your life. When making the choice to blame others for the situation, there is no personal accountability. You're basically saying "I'm helpless to their acts, actions and my reaction/s." This mindset is not true; there is always another option and choice you can make. Your actions are within your control and you decide if you're going to allow fear to run your life, or make a choice to live the cleanest life possible and act to your highest standards.

Do you remember the boxer analogy at the beginning of the book? The points in the previous questions will allow you to become trained. You'll leave behind the days when you simply reacted to the individual or situation. With practice, life's difficult situations will slow and some clarity will present itself. The long-term goal is to build a healthier life, relationship, and become closer to those important people in your life.

By now you've seen that it causes great harm mentally and physically. Plus, it eats away at the trust and safety needed in long-term relationships. It robs you of life's smallest and sweetest moments of potential. All due to perceived fear which our bodies and brains believe is danger.

Fight or Flight should not belong in your daily life.

CONCLUSION

 "I felt a sensation. Fight or flight. It's constant. I should just pick one. I, Elliot Alderson, am flight. I am fear. I am anxiety, terror, panic." Mr. Robot Season 1 E 6[1]

Fight or Flight! Make better decisions for your life is meant to be a call to action to live your life with more intention. Too often, we don't realize what habits run our lives until we stop and think about it, and decide to make different decisions. Wanting to read this book is already setting you to be in the right path to a better life.

It is only by training yourself to let logic remain in control that can you distinguish between true danger and simple fear, making a rational decision on how to proceed. It is a habit to see Danger where there is only Fear. It is a habit to see only two options when there are limitless possibilities. Today you can consciously choose to see only fear and see limitless possibilities.

Today you have the option to "train" yourself like the professional fighter, rather than leaving it up to your survival instincts. When you train, you can create your own experiences and make your life what you choose. The untrained individual, on the other hand, has a tough way forward through never-ending fears that hit him one after another.

You'll never be completely free of fear, and that's ok. I frequently feel fear, and that doesn't mean I'm doing anything wrong. What's important is to have the clarity to recognize that I'm not in a dangerous situation. I have developed the tools to analyze the circumstances and have confirmed the confidence that I'm in safe and trusting environments in my relationships and life. I also have the questions that help me to keep centered and trained to face any upcoming experiences that might trigger my Fight or Flight response. Today I'm trained, and when that happens, my life improves in every way and that's what **I want for you**.

Because of my training, I can feel my fears, and I move forward anyway. Fight or Flight is not running or ruining my life. I'm consciously in charge of where I'm going, what decisions I make, and how I act and react in my relationships. When Fight or Flight takes over, and I make a poor decision for myself or others, I don't give up and disengage. I apologize and rectify the situation for the sake of myself and others, and you will have that too.

I hope that the information and strategies in this book help you regain control of your life by regulating your Fight or Flight instincts and approaching stressful situations from a place of logic, rationality, and confidence. Are you ready?

---

1. Esmail, Sam (Director & Producer). (2015, July 29). Brave Traveler. [Television Series episode in] Mr. Robot. New York, New York: USA Network.

BIBLIOGRAPHY

Cannon, Walter Bradford, *Bodily Changes in Pain, Hunger, Fear and Rage: An Account of Recent Researches into the Function of Emotional Excitement, Reprint Edition*, FQ Legacy Books, 2010.

McGonigal, Kelly Ph.D., *The Upside of Stress: Why Stress is Good for You, and How to Get Good at It*, Reprint edition, Avery, 2016.

Sapolsky, Robert M., *Why Zebras Don't Get Ulcers: The Acclaimed Guide to Stress, Stress-Related Diseases, and Coping*, Third edition, Henry Holt and Company, 2004.

READING LIST - RESEARCH AND ARTICLES FOUND INSIGHTFUL

FEAR VS DANGER

Guthrie, Dana. (2014, October 22). Houston Chronicle. "Survey reveals America's biggest fears." http://www.chron.com/life/article/Survey-reveals-America-s-biggest-fears-5840250.php#photo-7033683 (Last Accessed: 2020, March)

FIGHT OR FLIGHT AND OUR HEALTH

Research and articles that do a good job of linking the two are:

Kiecolt-Glaser, J & Glaser, R. (2005, April 5). US National Library of Medicine. "How Stress Damages Immune System and Health."(abstract) https://www.ncbi.nlm.nih.gov/pubmed/20704904 (Last Accessed: 2020, March)

Pounds Marcia H. (2019, January 4). Sun Sentinel. "You knew hurricanes are stressful. Now researchers know how much." https://www.sun-sentinel.com/health/fl-bz-hurricane-stress-20190102-story.html (Last Accessed: 2020, March)

Thorn B.E., Pence L.B, et al. (2007, December). The Journal of Pain. "A Randomized Clinical Trial of Targeted Cognitive Behavioral Treatment to Reduce Catastrophizing in Chronic Headache Suffers." (Abstract) https://www.jpain.org/article/S1526-5900(07)00772-9/abstract (Last Accessed: 2020, March)

LONG TERM HEALTH IMPACT OF LIVING IN FIGHT OR FLIGHT

Keshner, Andrew. (2019, January). MarketWatch.com. "Income volatility and heart attacks may go hand-in-hand." www.marketwatch.com/story/income-volatility-and-heart-attacks-may-go-hand-in-hand-2019-01-07 (Last Accessed: 2020, March)

Harvard Health Publishing. (2018, May 1). "Understanding the stress response." www.health.harvard.edu/staying-healthy/understanding-the-stress-response (Last Accessed: 2020, March)

Shmerling, Robert. H. (2018, August 22) Harvard Health Publishing. "Autoimmune disease and stress: Is there a link?" https://www.health.harvard.edu/blog/autoimmune-disease-and-stress-is-there-a-link-2018071114230 (Last Accessed: 2020, March)

Huan Song, MD PhD, Fang Fang, MD, PhD, Gunnar Tomasson, MD, PhD; et al. (2018, June 19). JAMA Network. "Association of Stress-Related-Disorders with Subsequent Autoimmune Disease" (Abstract) https://jamanetwork.com/journals/jama/fullarticle/2685155

(Last Accessed: 2020, March)

Mannix, Liam. (2018, January 25). Sydney Morning Herald. "Chronic stress could rewire your brain to keep blood pressure high". https://www.smh.com.au/lifestyle/health-and-wellness/chronic-stress-could-rewire-your-brain-to-keep-blood-pressure-high-20180125-p4yyvl.html (Last Accessed: 2020, March)

Hall, Susan. (2013, June 7). Scott and White. "Fight or Flight? Our Reaction to Hight Blood Pressure" https://scrubbing.in/fight-or-flight-our-reaction-to-high-blood-pressure/ (Last Accessed: 2020, March)

The Washington Post, "Is Pessimism Bad for your Health." https://www.washingtonpost.com/archive/lifestyle/wellness/1996/05/14/is-pessimism-bad-for-your-health/c33a5831-791c-4a06-b192-31883cce5d58/ (Last Accessed: 2020, March)

Lawson, Kimberly. (2016, November 21) "How Pessimism can Impact your Health" https://www.vice.com/amp/en_us/article/mbqaky/how-pessimism-can-impact-your-health (Last Accessed: 2020, March)

Stahl, Stephanie. (2019, January 11). Philadelphia CBS. "Watching an Eagles Game is Literally a Workout, Doctors say" https://philadelphia.

cbslocal.com/2019/01/11/watching-an-eagles-game-is-literally-a-workout-doctors-say/ (Last Accessed: 2020, March)

BREATHE

Cuda, Gretchen. (2010, December 6) NPR (National Public Radio). "Just Breathe: Body Has A Built-In Stress Reliever." http://www.npr.org/2010/12/06/131734718/just-breathe-body-has-a-built-in-stress-reliever (Last Accessed: 2020, March)

GENERAL KNOWLEDGE

Goldstein, Michael. (2019, May 7). Forbes "After 900% Increase in 2018, Airline Fatalities Rising Again" https://www.forbes.com/sites/michaelgoldstein/2018/12/28/airline-fatalities-rise-more-than-900-in-2018/amp/ (Last Accessed: 2020, March)

Bureau of Transportation Statistics. (Date Accessed: 2019, March 23). Revenue Passenger-miles (the number of passengers and the distance flown in thousands (000)). https://transtats.bts.gov/data_elements.aspx?data=3 m (Last Accessed: 2020, March)

Made in the USA
Monee, IL
15 June 2020